Michael Price

Tablet PCs
for Seniors

Covers Windows RT and Windows 8 Tablet PCs

In easy steps is an imprint of In Easy Steps Limited
4 Chapel Court · 42 Holly Walk · Leamington Spa
Warwickshire · United Kingdom · CV32 4YS
www.ineasysteps.com

Notice of Liability
Every effort has been made to ensure that this book
contains accurate and current information. However, In
Easy Steps Limited and the author shall not be liable for
any loss or damage suffered by readers as a result of
any information contained herein.

Trademarks
Microsoft® and Windows® are registered trademarks
of Microsoft Corporation. All other trademarks
are acknowledged as belonging to their respective
companies.

In Easy Steps Limited supports The Forest Stewardship
Council (FSC), the leading international forest
certification organisation. All our titles that are printed
on Greenpeace approved FSC certified paper carry the
FSC logo.

FSC
www.fsc.org

MIX
Paper from
responsible sources
FSC® C020837

Printed and bound in the United Kingdom

ISBN 978-1-84078-586-9

Contents

1 Tablet PCs

This chapter examines how Tablet PCs have developed and evolved into the various types, discusses what's involved in selecting your Tablet PC, and looks in detail at Microsoft Surface, the example used in this book.

Tablet Computers

The Tablet computer is a device that is designed for mobility and use in a variety of situations where keyboards would be unsuitable or difficult to use. The devices are larger than cellphones or PDAs (personal digital assistants) and are integrated with a flat touchscreen. They are principally operated by touching the screen with a stylus, a digital pen or with fingers.

There's usually no physical keyboard, though they often use an on-screen virtual keyboard. Variations on the tablet form include hybrid computers with a detachable keyboard, convertible computers whose keyboards can be hidden by swiveling or sliding the screen, and computers with a keyboard connected by wireless link or USB port.

Tablet computers will use a variety of operating systems, including Android (Google), QNX (RIM) and iOS (Apple) as used in the Apple iPad. Such devices are used mainly for displaying published material such as videos, music, books and news. They are also used to create and exchange messages and photos through services such as Email, Facebook, Flickr and Twitter.

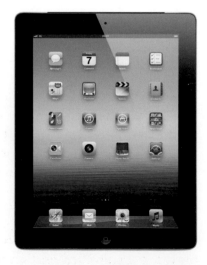

Tablet PCs on the other hand are full computers in tablet format, based on a multitasking operating system such as Windows or Linux. This allows support for functions such as creating documents, reports, spreadsheets and presentations. Microsoft initiated this approach with the Microsoft Tablet PC, a niche product used in hospitals and outdoor businesses. This used the Windows XP Tablet PC Edition which incorporated support for pen input.

Don't forget

The Home and Business editions of Windows Vista and Windows 7 provided a built-in set of Tablet PC functions, including the Tablet PC Input Panel.

6

Later releases of Windows did not have Tablet PC-specific editions of Windows but instead pen and touch support was built in to the main editions of the operating systems.

This approach has been continued with Windows 8, for Tablet PCs that are based on the standard Intel and AMD processors, as used for desktop and laptop computers. It also supports variations of these processors such as the Atom processor first used for Netbook PCs to improve battery life.

To further extend the battery life, there is an edition of Windows 8 specifically designed for Tablet PCs based on the ARM processor. This is known as Windows RT, and is provided preinstalled on PCs with ARM processors.

Hot tip

ARM processors use a RISC-based approach to computer design which results in lower costs, less heat, and less power usage. They are ideal for use in light, portable, battery-powered devices such as smartphones and tablets. Their use has now been extended to Tablet PCs.

Types of Tablet PC

Pure Tablet PC

The simplest form of Tablet PC consists of a touchscreen device that incorporates all the components, storage and connections and is preloaded with the operating system, either Windows 8 or Windows RT, depending on the processor type. There will be no physical keyboard, and you'd use the touchscreen for all input, with an on-screen virtual keyboard for text entry.

For example, the Asus VivoTab RT has a 10.1-inch, 1,366 x 768 pixel display and an Nvidia Tegra 3 (ARM class) processor. It comes with 2GB RAM and 32GB storage, and Windows RT and Microsoft Office RT are included. There's an 8-megapixel rear camera and a 2-megapixel front camera, and sensor support for orientation and direction.

The VivoTab is slightly larger, with 11.6-inch display (also 1,366 x 768 pixels) and features an Intel Atom (x86 class) processor, with 2GB RAM and 64GB storage. This machine has Windows 8 installed, but there's no edition of Microsoft Office included as standard. Like the RT model, there are front and rear cameras, and sensor support.

Hybrid Tablet, with Add-on Keyboard

Tablet PCs will usually be offered with some form of keyboard as a clip-on option. This may include other functions as with the Asus Tablet PCs, where the add-on keyboard provides additional battery power.

Other Tablet PCs may include the physical keyboard with the case, as with the Microsoft Surface Tablet PCs (see page 18). These offer two options, the Touch Cover with audio feedback and the Type Cover with physical buttons.

Such an option means the Tablet PC can be used as a hand-held device, or as a traditional laptop computer.

Don't forget

The add-on keyboard may also be used as a docking device to provide additional connections or to allow for extra storage.

Hot tip

Keyboards usually include a touchpad that operates as a mouse, controlling a pointer and providing two buttons giving left and right click functions.

Hot tip

The Touch Cover is ultra-thin to maximize portability. The Type Cover is thicker and has keys that move when they are pressed.

11

Convertible Computers

The convertible computer can be used as a Tablet PC or as a laptop, without having to remove the keyboard. The screen is rotated so that the keyboard is hidden and the computer can be operated by touch alone.

There are various mechanism for switching between tablet and laptop, depending on the manufacturers. For example:

Dell XPS 12 Convertible Ultrabook

This is a powerful machine featuring the latest Intel processors and having 4GB or 8GB RAM. There's also a 128GB or 256GB SSD (solid state drive), and the display is full HD (1920 x 1080 pixels).

The monitor frame allows the screen to swivel through 180 degrees, from tablet mode to laptop mode.

This computer comes with Windows 8 (64-bit edition), and there is no copy of Microsoft Office provided with the operating system.

Lenovo IdeaPad Yoga

The Lenovo IdeaPad Yoga comes in two models. The Yoga 13 has an Intel processor with up to 4GB RAM and 256GB SSD, and runs Windows 8. The Yoga 11 has an Nvidia ARM-class processor, with up to 2GB RAM and up to 64GB eMMC storage, and runs Windows RT.

Both models feature a 360 degree hinge that allows you to open the computer and select one of four modes – Laptop, Tablet, Tent or Stand, whichever suits your purpose.

Lenovo ThinkPad Twist

This is a more traditional convertible, using a single hinge and a spin round, fold down screen that allows laptop, tablet, tent and stand modes.

The ThinkPad Twist features an Intel processor with 4GB RAM and up to 500GB hard drive. The operating system installed is Windows 8 Pro 64-bit.

Windows 8 versus RT

There are three editions of Windows 8 for computers based on the Intel or AMD processors (until now the usual processors for Windows PCs) and these are provided in 32-bit and 64-bit versions. For PCs based on the ARM processor there is just one edition called Windows RT, currently available as a 32-bit version.

Windows 8

Windows 8 is the base or entry edition that is intended for consumers and contains the main features of Windows 8, including touchscreen and keyboard/mouse support, Windows 8 apps, Windows Store access, Internet Explorer 10, enhanced Task Manager and multi-monitor support.

Windows 8 Pro

Windows 8 Pro is the edition designed for advanced users and for business or technical professionals. It includes all the features in Windows 8 plus extra features for encryption, virtualization, PC management and domain connectivity. Windows Media Center is not included in any edition of Windows 8 but is available as a chargeable media pack add-on for Windows 8 Pro.

Windows 8 Enterprise

Windows 8 Enterprise is the edition for customers with Software Assurance agreements and includes all the features of Windows 8 Pro plus more features for the IT departments, to enable PC management and deployment, advanced security, virtualization and mobility. Unlike the Windows 8 and Windows 8 Pro editions it will not be supplied as a separate retail pack.

Windows RT

Windows RT is only available pre-installed on Tablet PCs and convertible computers powered by the ARM class of processor. It is designed to enable new thin and lightweight form factors with enhanced battery life. Windows RT includes Office RT with touch-optimized desktop versions of Word, Excel, PowerPoint and OneNote. It does not support conventional Windows desktop applications.

Don't forget

The ARM processor provides extended battery life, at the cost of some limitations on function and performance.

Don't forget

For the business user, the main choices are the Professional and the Enterprise editions.

Selecting your Tablet PC

When choosing your Tablet PC, you should first of all decide which edition of Windows 8 is necessary for your purposes, since this will have a major influence on the ranges of Tablet PC that might suit.

You'll need Windows 8 (and an Intel/AMD processor-based Tablet PC) if you want to run conventional Windows applications such as Adobe Photoshop or Windows Media Player or many of the Windows games, or if you want to add a full edition of Microsoft Office.

If you feel mobility and battery life are the most important issues, you could be satisfied with a Tablet PC that is ARM processor-based. This will have Windows RT plus Microsoft Office RT with its somewhat limited set of appplications.

If your requirements lie between these two positions, you should look at the hybrid Tablet PCs and the convertible PCs. These will give you a physical keyboard, either attachable or integrated. You'll normally be able to choose between models that run Windows 8 or Windows RT. You will find yourself trading off mobility factors such as weight and size against higher levels of memory and storage or additional connectivity options.

When you are reviewing your possible Tablet PCs, the questions that you should be asking include:

- What editions of Windows and Office does it run?

- What size and resolution is the screen?

- What connection does it offer, e.g. Wi-Fi or 3G/4G?

- How many cameras are there, and what size?

- How much RAM and storage space is offered?

- How thick is it, and what does it weigh?

We look at some of the Tablet PCs currently available, to see the range of features you can expect, and then look more closely at Microsoft Surface, used as the example system.

Don't forget

Existing versions may be for Windows 8 only, but you may find some Windows applications being re-issued in new versions that are designed for Windows RT.

Hot tip

In the following chapters, the Microsoft Surface Tablet is used to illustrate the options and actions discussed. However, the topics covered apply to any Tablet PC running Windows 8 or Windows RT.

Windows RT Tablet PCs

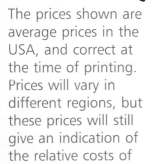

Don't forget

The Windows RT Tablet PCs feature Microsoft Office RT and are usually lower weight, with thinner profiles and longer life batteries because of the ARM processors.

Hot tip

The prices shown are average prices in the USA, and correct at the time of printing. Prices will vary in different regions, but these prices will still give an indication of the relative costs of the systems.

ASUS Vivo Tab RT — Tablet/hybrid

$599.00
10.1" screen, 8MP + 2MP cameras
Up to 8 hours battery life
1.15 lbs weight
10.33" x 6.71" x .33"
32GB/64GB storage
2GB memory
Nvidia Tegra 3 processor

Dell XPS 10 — Tablet/hybrid

$499.99 – 749.00
10.1" screen, 5MP + 2MP cameras
Up to 10 hours battery life
1.4 lbs weight
10.8" x 6.9" x .36" (+ .41" dock)
32GB SSD storage
2GB memory
Qualcomm S4 dual-core ARM

Lenovo IdeaPad Yoga 11 — Convertible

$799.00 – 899.99
11.6" screen, 720p HD webcam
Up to 13 hours battery life
2.8 lbs weight
0.66" thickness
64GB SSD storage
2GB memory
Nvidia Tegra 3 processor

Samsung ATIV Tab — Tablet/hybrid

$649.00
10.1" screen
8MP + 1.9MP cameras
8200 mAh battery
1.28 lbs
10.46" x 6.62" x 0.35
32GB–64 GB
2 GB
Qualcomm APQ8060A

Windows 8 Tablet PCs

ASUS Vivo Tab
Tablet/hybrid

$799.00
11.6" screen, 8MP + 2MP cameras
Up to 8 hours battery life
1.54 lbs weight
11.58" x 7.43" x 0.34"
64 GB eMMC
2GB
Intel Cloverview processor

HP Envy x2
Tablet/hybrid

$849.00
11.6" screen, 8MP + 1080p cameras
Up to 14 hours (tablet and base)
Tablet 1.54 lbs, total 3.13 lbs
11.92" x 8.11" x .37" (+ .39" base)
64GB eMMC storage
2GB memory
Intel Clover Trail SoC processor

Lenovo ThinkPad Tablet 2
Tablet

$699.00 – 799.99
10.1" screen, 8MP + 2MP cameras
Up to 10 hours
1.3 lbs weight
0.38" thickness
64GB SSD storage
2GB memory
Intel Clover Trail processor

Lenovo IdeaPad Yoga 13
Convertible

$949.00 – 1,000.00
11.6" screen, 720p HD webcam
Up to 8 hours battery life
3.09 lbs
0.67" thickness
Up to 256GB SSD
Up to 8GB
Up to Intel Core i7

Don't forget

The Windows 8 Tablet PCs are generally more powerful, but heavier and with lower battery life, though a second battery in the keyboard or docking unit can compensate for this.

Hot tip

Some Windows 8 Tablet PCs use versions of the Intel Atom, which is more power efficient than the Intel processors used in most laptop and desktop PCs.

Microsoft Surface

Microsoft has designed and marketed its own Tablet PCs – the Microsoft Surface for Windows RT and the Microsoft Surface for Windows 8 Pro. They are tablet format, with an integrated kickstand and an optional keyboard. This connects

magnetically to the tablet case and also acts as a cover for the screen. The magnetic connection handles the data transfer as you type. There are two versions – the Touch Cover and the Type Cover.

The thin case (0.37" for the RT model and 0.53" for the Pro) is still able to accommodate a full size USB port, and there are connections for a headset, an external display, the power supply adapter and the keyboard/cover, plus a microSDXC card slot.

The case also incorporates the volume and power buttons, and there's a Windows key on the front of the screen that performs the same functions as the Windows logo key on a standard PC keyboard.

Inside the case for either model there are sensors (ambient light, accelerometer, gyroscope and compass) and adapters for the Wi-Fi and Bluetooth wireless connections. There are also two 720p cameras, microphones and stereo speakers. However, there's a number of significant differences between the devices, including size, weight and screen resolution.

Surface RT	Surface Pro
Operating system	
Windows RT	Windows 8 Pro
Software	
Office 2013 RT	Windows Desktop apps
Size	
10.81 x 6.77 x 0.37	10.81 x 6.81 x 0.53 (ins)
27.45 x 17.19 x 0.93	27.45 x 17.29 x 1.32 (cms)
Weight	
1.5 lbs	2 lbs
676g	903g
Storage	
32GB, 64GB	64GB, 128GB
Memory	
2GB RAM	4GB RAM
Display	
10.6"	10.6"
ClearType HD	ClearType Full HD
1366 x 768 pixels	1920 x 1080 pixels
Multi-touch	
5-point	10-point
Pen Input	
Supported	Supported
No pen supplied	Inductive pen supplied
Processor	
Nvidia Tegra 3	3rd Gen Intel Core i5 with
Quad-core	Intel HD Graphics 4000
Battery	
31.5W-h	42 W-h
Up to 8 hours	4 to 5 hours estimated
Ports	
Full-size USB 2.0	Full-size USB 3.0
HD video out port	Mini DisplayPort
Power Supply	
24W power supply	48W power supply
	including 5W USB for
	charging accessories

Don't forget

Both models will run Windows 8 Apps from the Windows Store. Only the Pro model is able to run the Desktop Apps listed at the Windows Store or Windows applications available from the suppliers and developer websites.

19

Hot tip

Both models support a full size USB port that can handle most types of devices. However, only the Pro model can handle USB 3.0 devices or provide charging facilities for USB devices.

Don't forget

There are versions of these accessories available for the Surface RT and the Surface Pro. However, they are not generally interchangeable between the two.

Hot tip

If you want to plug in more than one USB accessory at once, for example a mouse and a printer, you should use a USB hub with its own power supply.

Accessories

Microsoft offers accessories for the Surface Tablet PCs, in addition to the Touch Cover and Type Cover. For example:

Surface HD AV Adapter

Designed to match the angled profile of the Surface PCs, this adapter lets you connect your Tablet PC to any HDMI-compatible display (HDTV, monitor, or projector) and stream movies, play video games and watch slideshows in high definition.

Surface VGA Adapter

This adapter lets you share your photos, video, and presentations by connecting the Tablet PC to VGA-compatible displays, monitors or projectors.

Both adapters are around 12" in length but need an HDMI or VGA extension cable as appropriate to complete the connection.

USB Devices

Microsoft Surface PCs include a full-size USB port, so you can add USB accessories such as a printer, camera, music player, a mouse, or even an external hard drive. You should confirm that the devices you want to use are compatible with Windows RT or Windows 8 as appropriate.

Wedge Touch Mouse

This is a special edition of the Wedge Touch Mouse Inspired by Surface. It is small enough to fit in your pocket, features a dark titanium finish and is easily paired with your Surface PC using Bluetooth technology.

MicroSDXC Memory Cards

The Surface tablets include a microSDXC card slot, and suitable memory cards are available from independent suppliers. The tablets can accept cards of up to 64GB to provide additional storage.

2 Using the Tablet PC

Start your Tablet PC for the first time, complete the setup then display the Start screen . From here you can start an app, display the Chams bar, Snap apps and visit the Desktop, using Touch gestures, Hotspots and shortcuts. Finally, you will learn how to close apps and shut down Windows.

Starting for the First Time

The first time you start the Tablet PC, you need to complete the initial setup, enter your details and set your preferences.

Don't forget

When the keyboard gets close to Surface, it clicks into place. It holds quite firmly, and can take the weight of the tablet. However, a sharp tug will easily detach it.

 If you have the Touch Cover or the Type Cover, use the magnetic link to attach it to your Tablet PC

Hot tip

The first time you switch on the Tablet PC, make sure you are connected to the mains supply. This prevents the system from running out of battery power during initial setup.

2 Flip out the kickstand on the back of the Tablet PC, plug the power cable into the mains and attach it magnetically to the Tablet PC

3 Press the power button on the top right of the Tablet PC, to start the system

4 The Tablet PC starts and Windows Setup loads, while the Logo and the Busy icon are displayed

5 When prompted, choose the language you'll want to see and use most on this computer, and tap Next

6 Read the license terms and tap the checkbox to accept the license terms, then tap Accept

7 Pick the color that you'd like for the Start screen, enter a name for the Tablet PC, and then tap Next

8 Tap your wireless network name, tap Connect then enter your password and tap Connect

Your Tablet PC will connect to your wireless network and then display the Settings screen.

9 Tap Use express settings to use the default settings or tap Customize to choose your settings

Complete the Setup

You'll be asked for an email address that will be used as a Microsoft account, to let you access the Windows Store, get online content and sync settings online.

1. Enter your preferred email address and click Next

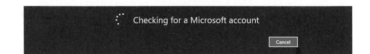

2. Windows checks the Microsoft account associated with that email address and asks for the password

3. Provide your security verification information (or check the details shown) and tap Next

4. To finish the setup, enter your date of birth and gender and then tap Next

5 Windows sets everything up, and shows a few messages as you wait for completion

While we're getting things ready

Check out the new way to use Windows

6 A small tutorial reminds you of how you can use the mouse (or Touch) to operate the Tablet PC

Move your mouse into any corner

7 Windows continues to work in the background

We're getting your PC ready

This will take a few minutes

8 Windows installs the initial set of Windows 8 Apps

Installing apps

This will take a few minutes

9 Finally, Windows displays the Start screen

The Start Screen

1 When initial setup completes, the Start screen is displayed, showing tiles for some installed apps

2 Slide your finger across the screen from right to left, to reveal the tiles for the remaining apps

3 If your system has Windows RT installed, you'll also have tiles for Office applications. Windows 8 systems require Office to be installed as a separate product

Get Started with Touch

With a Tablet PC, the main interface is through Touch:

When asked to		What you do	What happens
Tap		Tap once on an item	Opens the item that you tap
Press and hold		Press and hold your finger down for a few seconds	Shows options related to what you're doing
Slide		Drag your finger across the screen	Scrolls through what's on the screen
Pinch		Pinch thumb and forefinger together	Zooms out (shrinks image)
Stretch		Move thumb and forefinger apart	Zooms in (magnifies image)
Rotate		Put two or more fingers on an item and turn your hand	Rotates that item
Slide item a short distance		Tap and slide an item a short amount down	Selects that item
Slide to rearrange		Tap and drag an item to a new location	Moves that item
Swipe from edge		Swipe in from the edge of the screen	The action depends on the edge involved

Don't forget

In place of a finger use an inductive pen as supplied with the Surface Pro, or a capacitive pen such as the Logic Stylus with the Surface RT. This can be very useful when small target areas are involved.

27

Hot tip

Right edge:
Opens the charms bar
Left edge:
Switches between open apps and snaps apps side-by-side
Top or bottom edge:
Shows commands
Top edge:
Closes an app

Start an App

1. Press the Windows button (or the keyboard Windows key) to display the Start screen

2. Slide the screen if necessary to show the tile for the required app, then tap that tile

3. The app loads up with a full screen image, in this case weather details for the current location

4. Touch the Windows button to return to the Start screen and start another application, for example tap the tile for the Maps App

5 The new app opens full screen, overlaying the screen for the previously-displayed app

As you start more apps, the Desktop app included, each one will take over the whole screen, leaving all the other apps running in the background.

6 Swipe across the width of the screen from the left edge to switch to the next app in turn

7 Swipe a short distance to the right then back left, to reveal the Apps Switcher, to select a particular app

Hot tip

With the keyboard press WinKey (see page 35) + Tab to display the Apps Switcher. Alternatively, press Alt + Tab to show Windows 8 apps and Desktop applications. Repeat to go through the list and select the app you want.

29

Hot tip

With the mouse, move to the top left corner to display an app icon, then drag down to get the Apps Switcher. You can also go to the bottom left corner to display the Start icon, then drag up to get the Apps Switcher.

Charms Bar

From the right edge of the screen, you can display what's known as the Charms bar (due to its appearance).

1 Swipe to the left from the right edge, and the Charms bar appears with its five entries

Hot tip

You can use the pointer to reveal the Charms bar (see page 34)

2 The time and date are also displayed on the screen, along with icons for Wi-Fi and Battery status

The actions performed via these Charms are:

Find Apps, Settings and Files on Surface or search within an app such as Store or Music

Share Links, Photos and Files with your friends and with social networks from within the app

Go to the Start screen, or if you're already at the Start screen, go to the last app you were in

Send files and stream movies to TVs, printers and other devices

Change the Settings for Windows itself, or for the app from which the Charms bar is displayed

You can also press and hold the Windows logo key on the keyboard and then click C to display the Charms bar

Don't forget

You'll find a Charms bar at the top of the keyboard, if you have a Touch Cover or Type Cover for your Surface Tablet PC.

30

The Desktop

The Desktop is a Windows 8 App that runs conventional Windows applications such as Paint or Notepad, or any of the Office applications. To run a Desktop application:

1 Display the Charms bar, tap Search, then type the application name, e.g. Notepad, and tap Enter

Don't forget

With Windows RT, the Desktop is limited to a few applications. With Windows 8, you can run just about any Windows 7-compatible application.

2 The Desktop is displayed, and the named application is opened in a window on the desktop

Hot tip

You can tap the Desktop tile in the Start screen to open or switch to the desktop whenever you want.

3 You can access applications from shortcuts on the taskbar or the desktop, or run tasks from the icons in the Notification area, for example the Battery Status

Snap Apps

Windows 8 apps can be persuaded to share the screen with the Desktop or another app, using the Windows 8 Snap feature, as long as your monitor has the required resolution.

The minimum screen resolution to use the Windows 8 Snap feature is 1366 x 768.

To display the last-used app alongside the current app:

 Swipe from the left edge to select the last-used app, then release it when the Snap bar appears on the left

Hot tip

To snap a specific app, display the Apps Switcher, then slide the required app down a little (or right-click and select Snap left or Snap right).

The app is displayed in a narrow window to the left of the current foreground app

If you swipe further across until the Snap bar appears on the right, then release, the app snaps to the right

4. You can Snap the current app by pressing WinKey (see page 35) + Period. The app snaps right, snaps left and goes full screen, changing each time you press the keys

Don't forget

If you press WinKey + Shift + Period, the sequence becomes Snap left, Snap right, Full screen.

5. Use the App Switcher to select an app that will occupy the Fill view when you've set the Snap view

Hot tip

Drag to approximately one third or two thirds to Snap, or all the way to expand an app fully. Double-click the Snap bar to switch the Snap view left or right

6. Using the mouse or touch, drag the Snap bar across the screen to exchange the Snap and current apps

Hotspots

Windows 8 associates actions with Hotspots at the corners of the display when these are accessed by the mouse pointer or the Touchpad pointer.

Don't forget

Open the Desktop and start a couple of Windows 8 apps before you try out these hotspots.

1. Move the pointer to the top right or bottom right corner and the Charms bar will appear as an overlay

2. Move the pointer over any of the charms to activate the Charms bar and also display the time and date on the screen (see page 30)

3. From the Start screen, move the pointer to the top left or bottom left corner and a miniature of the last-accessed app is displayed. Click to switch there

Don't forget

Move the pointer up or down from the left thumbnail to display the Apps Switcher (see page 29).

4. From any app, move the pointer to the top left to display a thumbnail of the next previously-accessed app

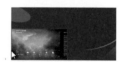

5. Move to the bottom left to display a thumbnail for the Start screen

6. From any screen, display the thumbnail at the lower left corner, and right-click to display the Quick Link menu (also known as the Power Users menu)

Keyboard Shortcuts

If you have a keyboard attached to your Tablet PC, you can use it to perform equivalent actions, pressing keys in combination with the Windows Logo Key (WinKey):

- **WinKey + C**   Display Charms bar
- **WinKey + D**   Display and hide the Desktop
- **WinKey + E**   Open Computer
- **WinKey + F**   Open Search charm for Files
- **WinKey + H**   Open the Share charm
- **WinKey + I**   Open the Settings charm
- **WinKey + J**   Switch the main and snapped apps
- **WinKey + K**   Open the Devices charm
- **WinKey + L**   Lock your PC or switch users
- **WinKey + M**   Minimize all Desktop windows
- **WinKey + O**   Lock the screen orientation
- **WinKey + R**   Open the Run dialog
- **WinKey + Q**   Open Search charm for Apps
- **WinKey + U**   Open Ease of Access Center
- **WinKey + W**   Open Search charm for Settings
- **WinKey + X**   Display the Quick Link menu
- **WinKey + Z**   Show commands available in app
- **WinKey + pause**   Display the Systems Properties dialog
- **WinKey + plus**   Zoom in
- **WinKey + minus**   Zoom out
- **WinKey + period**   Snap app to the right
- **WinKey + shift + period**   Snap app to the left

Close Apps

When you start a Windows 8 app it opens full screen and becomes the active foreground app. The previously-active app moves into the background and is usually suspended, remaining in memory but not using other system resources. If memory is required, Windows will terminate suspended apps, so there's no need to close an app when you've finished with it. However, if you do want to close an app:

 Tap and hold the top of the screen for the active app, and drag down all the way to the bottom

 As you drag, the screen is converted into a thumbnail then moves down to the bottom and shrinks further

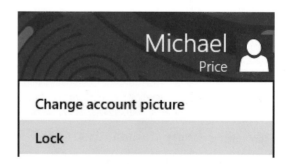

 As you complete the drag, the app is moved off the monitor, suspended for ten seconds and then closed

 The previously-active app is displayed full screen

You can close the active app using the mouse:

1 Move the mouse pointer to the top of the screen, where it becomes a Hand symbol

2 Drag the app down, as described for Touch, until the app moves off the screen to be suspended and closed

To close an app that's been suspended:

1 Display the Apps Switcher

2 Right-click the app to be removed, and select Close

3 Alternatively, touch and drag the app off the bottom of the screen

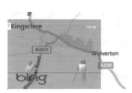

Don't forget

To close all of the background apps at once, select Settings from the Charms bar, tap or click Change PC Settings, General and then Delete history, to close all the suspended apps and remove them from memory.

Desktop apps retain all the conventional ways of closing. For example, to close File Explorer:

1 Touch and hold the titlebar and tap Close

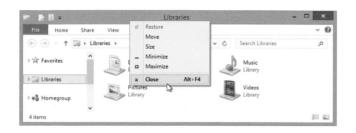

Hot tip

From the keyboard, you can also press Alt + F4 to close the selected desktop app.

2 Select File and Close   **3** Tap the Close button

37

Close Windows

With no Start button, there is no obvious way to close the Windows system, but there are several options you can use:

Ctrl + Alt + Del

1 Press the Ctrl + Alt + Del key combination

2 Tap the Power icon on the lower right and select one of the Close options, e.g. Sleep, Shutdown or Restart

Charm Settings

1 Display the Charms bar (see page 30) and select the Settings icon to display the Settings pane

2 Alternatively, you can press WinKey + I to display the Settings pane immediately

3 Tap the Power icon to display the Close options and select the one that's appropriate

Hardware Shutdown

On a portable PC you can close the lid, or press the power button to suspend operations or close the system down.

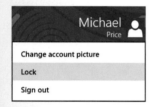

3 Working with Tablet PCs

Start your Tablet PC at the Lock and the Sign-on screens to enter your user name and password, and explore basics such as on-screen keyboard, Desktop and Standby modes, and the power options.

Starting Up

When you switch on your Tablet PC after the first time it displays the Lock screen, with the date and time, and perhaps some icons such as network and power status.

Hot tip

You can personalize the Lock screen and specify the background picture and the Quick Status icons displayed (see page 157).

1 Swipe up on a touch monitor to lift the Lock screen

Don't forget

Click the Lock screen with the mouse, or press any key on the keyboard to dismiss the Lock screen.

2 As you complete the swipe, the Lock screen is dismissed to reveal the sign-on screen

3 Type your Microsoft account password and Enter

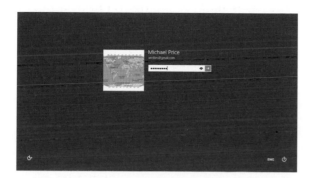

Don't forget

If your Tablet PC has no keyboard attached, the on-screen touch keyboard (see page 42) allows you to type the password.

4 The Start screen appears when sign-on completes, so you can select tiles to start Windows 8 apps

Hot tip

On the 1366 x 768 monitor, Windows RT displays three rows of tiles. On the same size monitor, Windows 8 displays four rows of slightly smaller tiles.

5 Select the Desktop tile to run File Explorer or an Office RT application, using the taskbar shortcuts

41

On-screen Keyboard

If you don't have a keyboard cover (or a USB keyboard) attached to your Tablet PC, the on-screen touch keyboard is used whenever text input is required. For example:

1 Select Search from the Charms bar and tap the text entry box to display the on-screen keyboard

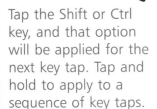
42

2 Tap alphabetic keys or select &123 to display the on-screen numeric keypad and the symbols

3 Tap the Faces key to display a set of icon symbols that might be useful for instant messages and emails

4 Tap the Keyboard button and select the Split keyboard, which is designed for typing with the thumbs

5 There's also a split Symbols & Numerics keyboard

6 Tap the Keyboard button and Input pad to enter text with a finger or a pen

7 This also has a numeric keypad and symbols option

Desktop Mode

When you select the Desktop app and enter desktop mode, you'll find that this also has an on-screen keyboard.

1 Start a desktop application such as Notepad that requires text input

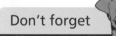

2 Tap the Keyboard icon on the right of the Taskbar

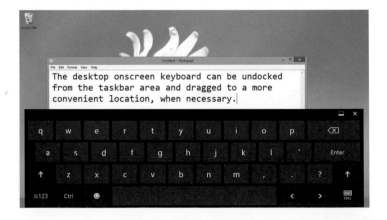

3 The on-screen keyboard is docked at the Taskbar, but you can tap and hold the top and drag to relocate it

4 As usual, tap the Keyboard button to change the type of keyboard or to remove it from the screen

Standby Mode

Whatever app is currently being displayed, if the Tablet PC is left without keyboard or touch intervention for a few minutes, the contents of the screen are cleared and the Tablet PC goes into Standby mode.

Hot tip

When the Tablet PC goes into Standby mode it remains connected to the Internet, waiting for you to wake it up and start using it again.

To wake up the system and redisplay the screen:

1. Press the Windows button, touch the power switch, press a key on the keyboard, or click a mouse button

2. The Lock screen is displayed, and you can swipe the screen, click the mouse or press any key

3. If standby was quite recent, the sign-on screen will appear briefly, but no password is called for
   or
   if standby has been for some time, the sign-on screen stays up for you to type your password

4. The previously-active app is displayed, and all other background apps will still be available

Don't forget

If you closed the cover, opening it will also wake up the system and display the Lock screen ready for you to sign on.

Saving Battery Power

The battery life (operating time between charges) is a key factor for Tablet PCs. Windows 8 and Windows RT are designed with this in mind, but you can take further steps to get the most out of the battery.

Choose an appropriate power plan

1 Windows 8 has two default plans
– Balanced (gives full performance when you need it)
– Power saver (reduces performance and brightness)

2 Tablet PCs with Windows RT have the Balanced power plan only (but you can still customize this)

Reduce display brightness

The display can use more power than any other part of your Tablet PC. To change the display brightness:

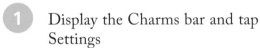

1 Display the Charms bar and tap Settings

2 Tap Brightness to make the change you want

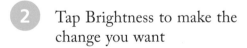

3 You can also tap the Battery icon on the Taskbar and select Adjust screen brightness

This opens the Power Options where you can make this and other adjustments to conserve the power available from your battery.

Switch to Standby Mode

If you know you won't be using your Tablet PC even for a brief period of time you can save power by closing the cover or tapping the power switch to tell Windows to put the system into standby mode immediately.

Power Options

There are several ways by which you
can display the power options panel for
your Tablet PC:

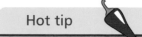

Hot tip

Note that this is a
Windows 8 system
with two power plans
offered.

1 Tap the Battery icon in the
Notification area of the taskbar
and select More power options

2 Display the Charms bar, select Search and Settings,
type Power Options and select this from the results

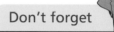

Don't forget

You can also open the
Control Panel, select
System and Security
and then select Power
Options, or open the
Quick Link menu (see
page 34) and select
Power Options.

The content of the Power Options panel depends on which
system you are running. With Windows 8, you'll normally
see the two power plans, Balanced and Power saver.

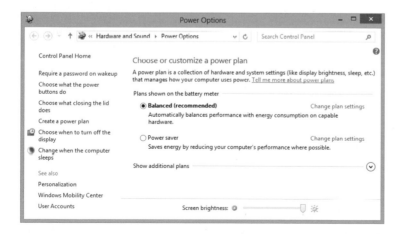

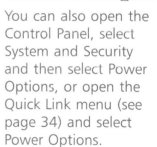

You can also show additional plans, to reveal the High
performance (but power intensive) plan plus any custom
power plans you may have created.

...cont'd

With Windows RT systems, there is only the Balanced plan listed and there are no additional plans to show.

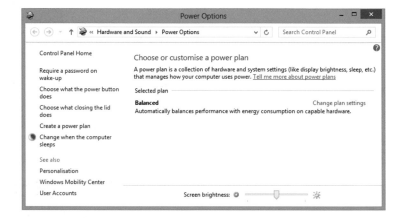

To make changes to any of the power plans on your system:

1. Select the power plan you want to change (if there's more than one) and tap Change plan settings

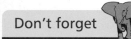
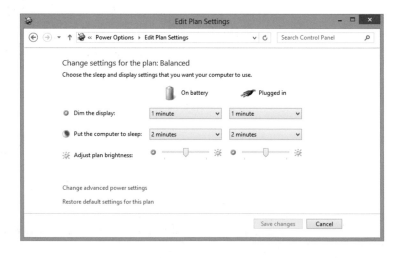

2. You choose delay values (from 1 minute to 5 hours) or specify Never, for dimming or for sleep mode

3. To make other changes select Change advanced power settings and review the options offered

Settings

The settings available will vary considerably, depending on the type of system and its attachments.

1. Windows RT systems will typically offer settings for desktop, power buttons and lid, display and battery

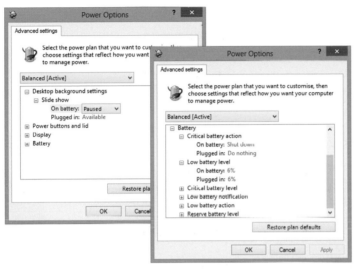

Don't forget

Expand the categories to see the settings and expand them to see the options and alternatives available.

For example, the battery section provides the trigger levels for notification to be given and action to be taken when the battery power is at a low or critical level

2. Systems that are Windows 8-based may have further components that can be managed

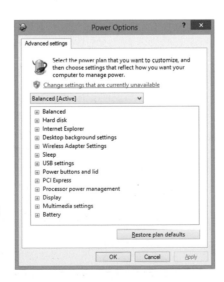

In this example, there are options for the hard disk, the browser, the wireless adapter, USB and processor and other items, in addition to the settings normally covered for Windows RT systems, as shown above.

Hot tip

You can experiment with the settings, and then select Restore plan defaults to undo all the changes and return the settings to their original values.

Power Supply Adapter

Unlike many laptop PCs, the Tablet PC batteries are not removable, so you can't keep a spare battery ready charged and available as a substitute for a discharged battery.

If you need to carry out a task that you cannot afford to be interrupted, for example applying a major update to your Windows system or taking a full backup, you need to be cautious. It is best not to rely on the battery to provide all the power needed, since there's a danger it could fail before the process ends. For such situations, you should attach the power supply adapter, and complete the task with the Tablet PC running under mains power.

The power adapter supplied with your Tablet PC will have a power plug appropriate to your region, but the adapter will be able to handle multiple voltages. There is a five-pin magnetic connector on the end of the cable. This is reversible and attaches to the Tablet PC in two ways, either cable up or cable down.

You can use the power adapter just to recharge the battery, which takes two or three hours for a fully-discharged battery, or you can continue using the machine, with charging continuing, though perhaps at a slower rate.

Click the Battery Status icon in the Notification area on the Desktop to confirm that your Tablet PC is charging. There's also a small neon light on the end of the connector.

51% available (plugged in, charging)

Adjust screen brightness
More power options

4 Tablet PC Software

Your Tablet PC has many preinstalled apps (programs) using the new Windows style. It also has access via the Windows Store to thousands of apps in over 20 categories. We use the Kindle app to illustrate the install procedures, and also look at Desktop apps for Windows 8 users.

Types of Programs

There are two basic types of program (app) that can be used on your Tablet PC – Windows 8 apps and Desktop apps.

Windows 8 Apps

Windows 8 features a new class of applications that are particularly designed for Tablet PCs and touchscreens. The active Windows 8 app occupies the full screen, except when using Windows 8 Snap (see page 32). Other Windows 8 apps run in the background but may be suspended if the system resources are required for the active tasks.

Desktop Apps

These are effectively conventional Windows applications that share the desktop environment. The applications that you can use depends on which edition of Windows 8 you have.

For Tablet PCs running Windows RT, there's only a limited number of such apps. These are pre-installed on the system and include a number of Windows utilities plus a special edition of Microsoft Office 2013.

Tablet PCs with Windows 8 have the Windows utilities but no edition of Microsoft Office. However, you can install just about any application that runs under prior versions of Windows, including various editions of Microsoft Office.

1 To view the installed apps, swipe up from the bottom edge of the screen and tap the All apps button

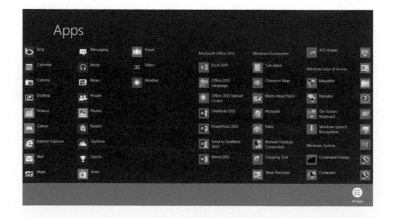

Preinstalled Programs

The apps preinstalled on your Tablet PC will include:

Bing	Games	Music	Sports
Calendar	Internet Explorer	News	Store
Camera	Mail	People	Travel
Desktop	Maps	Photos	Video
Finance	Messaging	SkyDrive	Weather

All these apps are represented by tiles on the Start screen.

Don't forget

Your Start screen may show other apps installed, or the tiles may have been rearranged.

This is the initial Windows RT Start screen. If you have Windows 8 there are normally no tiles for Microsoft Office.

Windows 8 and Windows RT systems also include the Reader app which allows you to view PDF and XPS documents. This app is normally hidden from view, with no Start menu tile. However, it can easily be invoked by selecting and opening a file of the associated type. You can view its description in the Windows Store.

Hot tip

Note that the Install button is replaced by a message saying that you own this app.

Windows Store

To search for, download and install Windows 8 apps to your Tablet PC you must visit the Windows Store.

 Select the Start screen and tap Windows Store

The Windows Store opens and displays Spotlight apps plus links to Top Free and New Releases

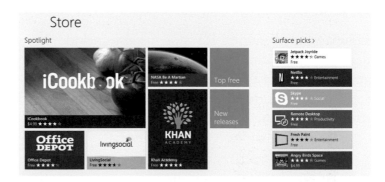

Swipe right to left to display Recommended, Top free and New releases for the 20 categories

...cont'd

4 Choose a category such as Books & Reference and tap the Top free button

5 Links are displayed for the relevant apps

 **Hot tip**

Tap New releases to see chargeable as well as free apps, or tap a recommended entry to display its details.

Top free in Books & Reference 100 apps

6 Tap a link, for example Encyclopaedia Britiannica, to read the overview

 **Don't forget**

For apps that you need to purchase, you'll see the Buy button rather than the Install button.

7 Select Details or Reviews for more information

8 Tap Install to add the app to your system and your Start screen

Explore Windows Store

You can search the Store to find apps that might be useful, using keywords related to the topic that interests you.

 With the Windows Store open, display the Charms bar and tap the Search button

Type the search term, for example, "cards"

Tap the Search button and matching apps are displayed

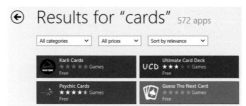

To get more exact matches, tap the All Categories box and select a specific category for example Games

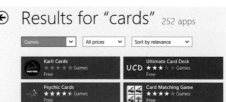

If you want business or greetings cards rather than playing cards, try selecting the Productivity category

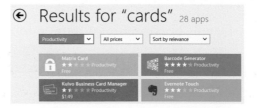

The apps in the Windows Store are divided into 20 different categories. To get an idea of the number of apps available in any one category:

1 Open the Windows Store and search for apps using a category name, for example Entertainment

Don't forget

The numbers of apps returned by any search will vary on a day-to-day basis, as apps are added to (or removed from) the Windows Store.

2 In this search 3554 apps for Windows RT are listed

Even though you search by category name, you may get apps in a variety of categories, since the search term can appear in the descriptions of apps in other categories.

3 Select the specific category from the category list, to restrict the list to that category – a total of 2999 apps

Beware

A complete search of the store (see page 58) found 3600 entertainment apps for Windows RT on that day, so not all such apps are found when you use the category name to search.

Repeat the search for other topics that may interest you. Categorization is not always exact, so a series of related searches can help to ensure that you find relevant apps.

Windows Store Categories

58

There's a quick way to calculate the numbers of apps that are available in the Windows Store in your region at any given time. Carry out a search using your Windows RT or Windows 8 system, with * as the search field.

Search for * in	Windows RT	Windows 8
Apps found	27850	23536

If you filter the search for each category in turn, you will get an idea of the overall distribution of apps in the store – on that day and for your location. The following list gives an indication of the numbers of apps in each category.

Categories	Windows RT	Windows 8
Games	3698	4702
Social	524	461
Entertainment	3600	2817
Photo	570	575
Music & Video	1017	985
Sport	816	647
Books & Reference	3163	1714
News & Weather	1599	994
Health & Fitness	875	689
Food & Dining	756	488
Lifestyle	1300	931
Shopping	179	147
Travel	1053	877
Finance	359	284
Productivity	1158	1174
Tools	2394	2214
Security	135	175
Business	709	391
Education	3835	3187
Government	110	84

Install Kindle App

1 Explore the Store to locate items of interest. For example search the Store for items related to ebook

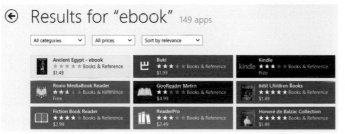

Don't forget

This search for eBook locates 149 apps for Windows RT and 160 apps for Windows 8, in Books & Reference, Productivity and Tools categories.

2 From the results, tap the app you want, e.g. Kindle

Hot tip

Once you've installed the app, you'll see a message saying that You own this app, if you review the app at the Store.

3 Tap Install to add this app to your Tablet PC

4 Messages at the Store show the installation in progress and tell you when it is completed

5 A tile for the new app is added to the Start screen

Run the App

1 Go to the Start screen, and tap the new tile for the app that you have added, e.g. Kindle

2 Tap Sign In, enter the email address and password for your Amazon account then tap the Sign in button

3 Tap Cloud to access the Kindle books you have previously purchased

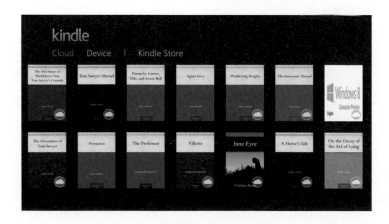

Your Kindle books are accessed over the Internet from Amazon's server, but you can store them on your Tablet PC to read offline.

1. Select a book and tap Download book on the App bar that appears

2. The App bar changes to offer the Cancel option, and the book is downloaded

3. Tap Device to view the list of books that are stored and available on your Tablet PC

4. Select Kindle Store to go to your local Amazon website to review and purchase additional books using your Kindle account

61

When you purchase a book you can choose Deliver to a specific Kindle device or to a Kindle app, and it will be stored at that location, as well as in the Cloud.

Read eBooks

1. Double tap the book (or select the book and tap Open on the App bar)

2. The book opens at the initial location or at the last location used

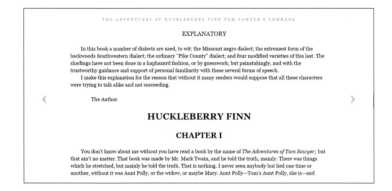

3. Tap to the right to advance, or to the left to go back

4. Swipe down from the top edge or up from the bottom edge to display the App and Progress bar

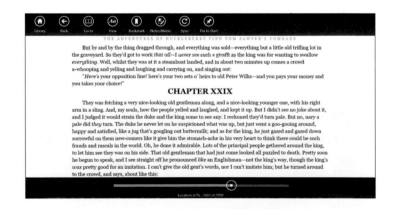

5. Tap the Library button to select a different book

Update Apps

If any of the installed apps have changes, an
indicator on the Store tile tells you how many
such updates you have waiting.

1. Touch the tile to open the Windows Store and you'll
   see a message to the same effect at the top right

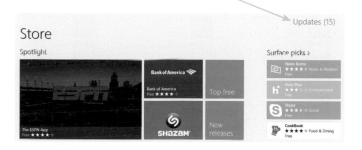

2. Tap the Updates message and you'll see a list of the
   apps for which updates are available

3. The updates are preselected, but you can touch to
   deselect any of the apps you don't want to install yet

4. Click Install to begin applying the selected updates

Hot tip

The updates are
for those apps you
install yourself as well
as those that were
initially included on
your system.

Don't forget

Tap Clear, then select a
single update, and the
View Details button
will be added. This
gives access to the
App Description, as
displayed when you
select the app at the
Store (see page 86).

...cont'd

(5) Several apps may be processed simultaneously, and you'll see a progress report for each update showing the stages: Pending, Downloading and Installing

(6) As updates are completed, the associated apps are removed from the list

(7) When all the stages are complete for all the items, you will be told that your apps were installed

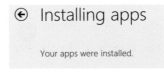

Desktop Apps

Windows Store also has entries for Desktop apps. These are conventional Windows applications that are run in the traditional desktop environment. You will often come across these as you search for Windows 8 apps. For example:

1. Search the Store Windows using the term "Desktop"

2. If your system is Windows RT, you get the usual mix of apps. These example results show 354 in total

3. With Windows 8, there are 350 normal apps which are supplemented by 101 identified as Desktop apps

4. Filter the results by the various pricing options

Pricing option	Windows RT	Windows 8	Desktop
All prices	354	350	101
Free	224	220	30
Free and trial	220	268	29
Paid	130	136	65

Run searches on other topics and scan for any Desktop apps.

Hot tip

Systems with Windows RT cannot run Desktop apps, so the Store will not show them unless the system doing the search is running an edition of Windows 8.

65

Hot tip

To locate Desktop apps you have to scan your results list manually and pick out the entries with Desktop app in place of the price (or Free marker).

Examples of Desktop Apps

Games
Age of Empires Online
Games App Desktop
Social
SmallCal
Entertainment
Corefx Creative
Ultra Screen Saver Maker
Photo
Adobe Photoshop
Ashampoo Snap 6
Corel Paintshop Pro
Crayola Art Studio
Instagrille
Picture Dude Image
QuickCrop
Serif PhotoPlus X5
SimplePics
SpotEasy
Music & Video
Ashampoo Slideshow
Audials One 9
ColorDirector
Moyea PPT to Video
Mp3 TrueEdit
Vid2Pics
News & Weather
Terminator
Productivity
Adobe Reader X
Construct 2
DriveHQ Online Backup
eDoc Organizer
Evernote Desktop
Gmail Notifier Pro v4.3.1
Microsoft Office 2010
Microsoft SkyDrive
NoteFlush

Pinch
Soluto Desktop
Team Viewer
Tools
BootRacer
CSignHelper
DeskOne
Emcee Desktop Organizer
GameMaker: Studio
gExplore
Image to PDF Converter
KAR Energy Software
Mikogo
Pokki Start Menu Win 8
Serial Port Monitor
StartFinity
Windows Location Tracker
Security
mSecure for Desktop
FastAccess Face Recog
Norton Antivirus
Business
Adobe Creative Cloud
Adobe Flash Pro CS6
Adobe InDesign CS6
FastDocument
IPSmith
Rollerscript
SecureZIP for Windows
Serif PagePlus Starter
Serif PagePlus X6
Serif WebPlus X6
WhizFolders Organizer
Education
Jumpstart Adv Preschool
Jumpstart Adv K-2 Train
Jumpstart Adv K-2 Quest
Jumpstart Adv 3-5

Review and Install

1 Search the Store for apps related to Adobe reader

2 In this case nine out of 14 are Desktop apps. Tap the entry for Adobe Reader XI to display its details

3 Select the link to Go to Publisher's website, clear the box for Google Chrome, and select Download now

If you carry out this search on a Windows RT machine, you'll find five PDF-related apps, but no Desktop apps.

You cannot purchase Desktop apps from the Windows Store – it just provides a link to the publisher's website.

...cont'd

Don't forget

You do not have to go via the Windows Store to download and install a conventional Windows application such as Adobe Reader. You can go direct to the publisher's website.

4 Follow the prompts to download and run the Adobe Reader setup program and install the application

5 A tile is added to the Start screen, and a shortcut is placed on the Desktop

Hot tip

Adobe Reader replaces the Reader app (see page 53) as default for file type PDF. Press and hold or right-click the file icon to display the menu and select Open with, to use the Windows 8 app or to reset the default.

6 Tap either of these to start the Adobe Reader on the Desktop

5 More Windows Software

Your Tablet PC has many Windows accessories. Windows RT users also have Office 2013 RT preinstalled. Windows 8 users can add the full Office and many more apps.

Windows Accessories

Windows 8 contains a number of the Windows accessories featured in previous versions and these run on the Desktop.

Hot tip

Windows RT systems do not include these accessories:
Sound Recorder
Sticky Notes
Windows Fax and Scan
Windows Journal
Windows Media Player
WordPad

1 Swipe up from the bottom edge of the Start screen and tap the All apps button

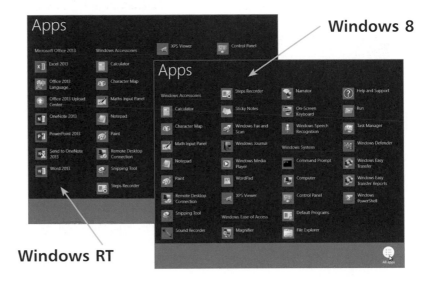

Windows 8

Windows RT

2 There are 12 Windows System apps, 4 Ease of Access, 9 Windows Accessories (15 for Windows 8) and 7 Microsoft Office 2013 (Windows RT only)

Hot tip

You can also type the accessory name on the Start screen, or pin the accessory to a tile or the Taskbar (see page 44).

3 Tap several accessories in turn to start them on the Desktop, where they can be resized or minimized

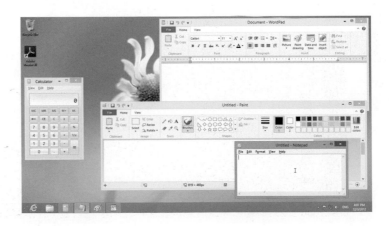

...cont'd

To play music files on your Windows 8 Tablet PC:

1 At the Start screen type media and select Windows Media Player which starts up on the Desktop

Alternatively, you can use the Music app:

1 On the Start screen, locate and select the tile for the Music app

2 When Xbox Music displays, select My Music

Don't forget

Your Tablet PC with Windows 8 has two options for playing music – Windows Media Player and the Music app. However, for your Windows RT Tablet PC, the Music app is the only option that is supported.

71

Hot tip

The Music app will play the files in your Music library and from the Xbox Music Store. Free use is limited to 10 hours a month after six months. It is unlimited with the Music Pass, and you can download and play tracks offline.

Xbox Music Pass
Try it free.

Microsoft Office 2013 RT

Hot tip

The Microsoft Surface with Windows RT was originally shipped with preview copies of the Office 2013 apps. If you still have the preview installed, you can use Windows Update (see page 178) to switch to the final version.

Don't forget

You can store your office documents on the hard drive on your Tablet PC, or on the SkyDrive that's associated with your Microsoft account. However, you cannot sync your SkyDrive files with local copies since that needs a Desktop app (see page 75).

Microsoft Office 2013 RT is a special version of Microsoft Office 2013 Home & Student edition. It is preinstalled on Tablet PCs and is optimized for these machines, to reduce battery usage, enable touch mode by default to improve usability on tablets, and use the graphics device for hardware acceleration.

To save disk space, templates, clip art and language packs are held online rather than being stored locally. There is no support for third-party code such as macros, VBA and ActiveX controls.

To start an Office RT application:

1. From the Start screen select the appropriate tile, e.g. Word 2013

2. From the Taskbar on the Desktop, select the application shortcut for Word 2013

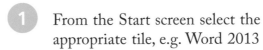

3. The application starts, ready for you to open a document

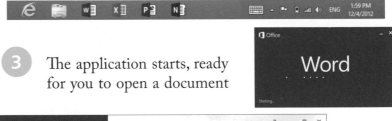

...cont'd

The applications in Office 2013 have been optimized for touch. To see how this is achieved:

1 Select Home on the Tab bar in Word 2013 and observe the layout of the Ribbon

2 Select the Touch/Mouse Mode button on the Quick Access toolbar to display the menu

3 The ribbon is in Touch mode so select the Mouse mode entry

4 The buttons and commands on the ribbon are re-arranged into a more tightly-fitted pattern

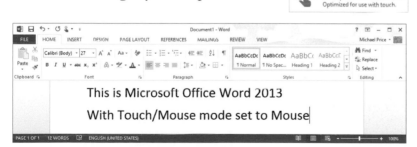

Other touch-related features being introduced include the Radial Menu as used in the Windows 8 app version of OneNote, which puts the commands at your fingertips.

Hot tip

If the ribbon is not displayed, touch and hold the Tab bar and tap the option Collapse the Ribbon to clear the tick mark.

Don't forget

If there's no Touch/Mouse Mode button on the Quick Access toolbar, touch the down-arrow at the right of the toolbar and select Touch/Mouse Mode to add a tick to that entry and display that button.

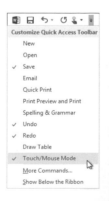

73

Microsoft Office 2013

If you have Windows 8 on your Tablet PC, you won't find a copy of Microsoft Office installed by default. However, you can install any edition of Microsoft Office 2013, including:

The tiles that you'll see on your Start screen depend on which edition of Office 2013 you have installed.

- Office 2013   Excel, OneNote
  Home & Student   PowerPoint, Word

- Office 2013   Excel, OneNote, Outlook
  Home & Business   PowerPoint, OneNote

- Office 2013   Access, Excel, OneNote, Outlook
  Professional   PowerPoint, Publisher, Word

- Office 2013   Access, Excel, InfoPath, Lync,
  Professional Plus   OneNote, Outlook, PowerPoint,
                Publisher, Word

When you install an edition of Office 2013 on your Windows 8 system, the application tiles will be added to the Start screen. To start an Office 2013 application:

74

1   From the Start screen select the appropriate tile, e.g. Excel 2013

When Office 2013 is installed, shortcuts aren't placed on the Taskbar, but you can add them:

The Apps screen shows numerous functions and utilities for Office 2013, in addition to the applications themselves.

2   On the Start screen, swipe up from the bottom edge to display the app bar

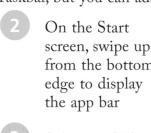

3   Select an Office 2013 app and tap Pin to taskbar

4 Repeat to add shortcuts for other applications

5 Select the Desktop and choose the shortcut for the app you want to run, e.g. Excel

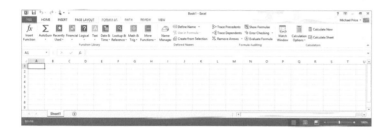

6 Display the applications in Touch mode or choose Mouse mode to leave more room for data

You can store your documents on your computer or on your SkyDrive.

With Windows 8, you can install the Microsoft SkyDrive. This is a Desktop app that creates a SkyDrive folder on your computer. Everything you store in this folder is automatically kept in sync with your SkyDrive on the Internet.

Microsoft SkyDrive
★★★★☆ Productivity
Desktop app

SkyDrive desktop app for Windows

Hot tip

Add shortcuts for the Office applications that you'll use often, for example Word, Excel, PowerPoint, OneNote and Publisher.

75

Don't forget

Microsoft SkyDrive allows you to work with your files locally but access them from anywhere that you sign on with your Microsoft account.

Windows Essentials

For Windows 8, the Windows Essentials collection gives you some useful Desktop applications. To install these programs:

1 Select Internet Explorer from the Start screen and type **windows.microsoft.com/en-US/windows-live/essentials-home**

windows.microsoft.com/en-US/windows-live/essentials-home

2 Scroll down and select the Download now button

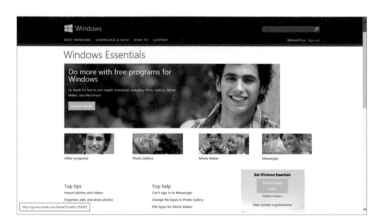

3 Select Run to download and install the program

4 When prompted, select Yes to allow the program to make changes to your system

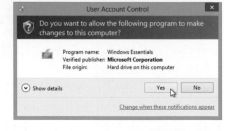

...cont'd

5 Choose to install all of Windows Essentials

Hot tip

You may be prompted to allow additional Windows features such as Microsoft Net Framework, that may be needed to operate Windows Essentials.

6 The components of Windows Essentials will be downloaded and installed in turn

77

7 The activity is displayed as a progress bar. Select Show Details to see the action by program

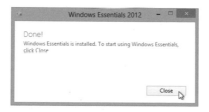

8 When installation completes, tiles for the applications are added to the Start screen

Don't forget

The original name for Windows Essentials was Windows Live Essentials. The programs still carry their old titles, though this may change in future updates.

Hot tip

If you have the base edition of Windows 8, you can purchase the Windows 8 Pro Pack to upgrade and add the Media Center.

Windows Media Center

Windows Media Center (WMC) is a digital video recorder and media player that allows you to view and record live television, as well as organize and play slideshows, music and videos. You can stream television programs and films through services such as Netflix.

WMC has been included as a feature in previous releases of Windows. For Windows 8 it is now provided as an add-on that can be applied to the Pro edition only. It is not available for Windows RT.

To add Windows Media Center to your Windows 8 Pro:

1 Swipe in from the right edge of the screen and tap Search, then type add features in the Search box

2 Tap Settings and select Add features to Windows 8

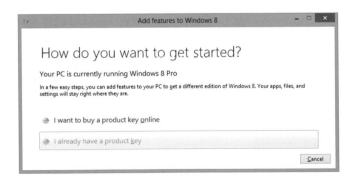

3 Select I want to buy a product key online to be prompted through the steps to buy a product key, and it will be entered for you

4 Alternatively, you could select I already have a product key, enter your product key and tap Next

5 Read the license terms, select the check box to accept the license terms, and then click Add features

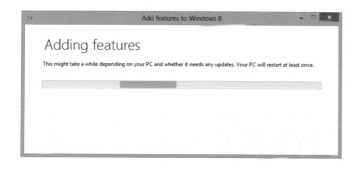

6 Your computer may restart several times while the updates are applied and the system is reconfigured

Starting WMC

If you are running Windows 8, your PC will finally restart with both Windows 8 Pro and Media Center installed.

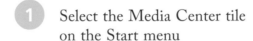

If you are running Windows 8 Pro, your PC will restart automatically and Windows Media Center will be installed and available for use.

To start Windows Media Center:

1. Select the Media Center tile on the Start menu

2. Select Continue and then Express to get started with Media Center using recommended options

Windows Downloads

You can find ways to personalize your computer and make it easier to use, at the Windows website

1 From the Start screen, select Internet Explorer and go to the website **windows.microsoft.com**

Don't forget

The downloads at the Windows website are available for computers with Windows 8 or with Windows RT.

2 Select Download & Shop to see what options are available for downloading to your computer

Hot tip

This web page also gives you information about Tablet PCs and other computers that can run the latest version of Windows.

3 Select the Free Downloads option and you can choose to personalize your PC, share music and photos or add security and utilities

...cont'd

Themes

Compatible with Windows 8 & Windows RT

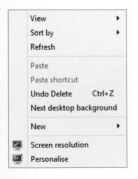

You can also display Personalization from the Control Panel (see page 167).

 4 Tap Personalization Gallery and then Themes to explore the categories

 5 Tap Details for a description of a theme, for example Caribbean Shores

6 Tap Download theme and then Open to transfer the associated files to your computer and allow Personalization to apply the theme to your Desktop

Other Windows Applications

Many applications written for previous versions of Windows will also run on Windows 8 (though not on Windows RT). To check if a particular application will work, you can visit the Windows Compatibility Center.

1 Select Internet Explorer from the start screen and type the address **www.microsoft.com/compatibility**

2 The Compatibility Center opens with Windows 8

3 Scroll down to see the popular products that have been rated as compatible with Windows 8

Hot tip

Select the arrow next to Windows 8 and choose Windows RT to explore compatibility of products with that system.

Hot tip

With Windows RT selected you'll have a different set of popular products listed.

Select Windows 8, type an application name, e.g. Adobe InDesign CS6 and tap or click Search

 Adobe InDesign CS6 is found to be compatible

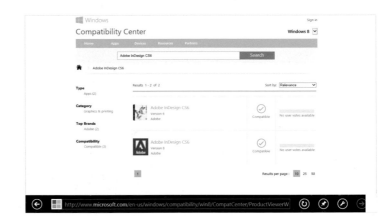

Switch to Windows RT, repeat the search and you find no compatible versions of InDesign CS6

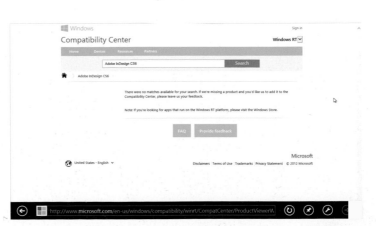

6 Email and Messaging

Send and receive emails with the Mail app, keep track of your contacts with the People app, have instant communication with the Messaging app, manage your meetings and your tasks with the Calendar app (or try Desktop equivalents on Windows 8 systems).

Apps for Email

Previous versions of Windows included applications for electronic mail and communication, such as Outlook Express, Windows Mail and Windows Messenger. There were also applications for managing contacts and calendars. These are no longer included, but Windows 8 and Windows RT have a set of apps that provide the equivalent functions.

These are preinstalled, but to get an overview, you can look in the Windows Store.

1 Visit the Windows Store, select Search and type Mail to find apps related to this topic

2 Locate the app entitled Mail, Calendar, People and Messaging and select that entry to see the details

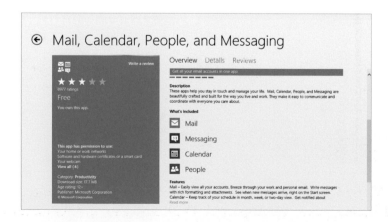

3 The item provides four apps associated with email

Don't forget

If you are running Windows 8 you can install the Windows Essentials (see page 76) to get Desktop apps for email and instant messaging. With the appropriate edition of Microsoft Office 2013 installed, you can use Outlook 2013 (see page 102).

Hot tip

If the Mail, Calendar... entry isn't immediately evident, select the Productivity category to reduce the number of apps in the results list. When you are able to select this item and view the description, you'll see that you already own this app.

Mail App

To start sending and receiving email in
Windows 8 or Windows RT:

1 Select the tile for the Mail app on
the Start screen

2 The first time, you are prompted for
the password for the email account
defined as your Microsoft account

Hot tip

The other apps that
are supplied along
with the Mail app are
also displayed on the
Start screen.

Add your Google account

To finish setting up this account, enter your password.

Email address

win8ies@gmail.com

Password

•••••••••

☑ Include your Google contacts and calendars

Connect   Cancel

3 Tap Connect to add the account, and the contents of
the Inbox and the latest messages are displayed

Hot tip

As noted at the foot
of the Accounts pane,
you go to Settings and
choose Accounts, to
define additional email
accounts. Click OK to
remove this message.

With higher resolution monitors, Accounts, Folder and
Reading panes are displayed. With lower resolution monitors
you get just Folder and Reading. Tap the
arrow to show Accounts and Reading.

  Gmail Inbox

Add Email Accounts

If you have other email accounts, you can add them to the Mail app, and view all your messages in one place. As already noted, you use the Mail Settings to define the additional accounts.

1　From Mail, display the Charms bar and select Settings (or press the WinKey + I)

2　From Settings, select the Accounts entry

3　From the Accounts list select Add an account

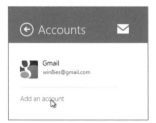

The Mail app supports a variety of account types, including Hotmail, Outlook, Google, AOL and Yahoo!

4　Choose the account type, e.g. Yahoo!

5　Enter the email address and password for the account

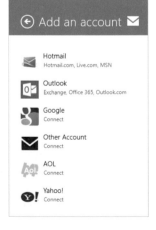

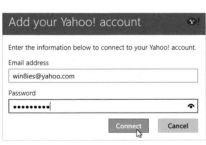

6　Click Connect, and Mail will define the account and set up the appropriate folders

If your email account type is not listed:

1 Select the type as Other Account, and enter the
email address and account number

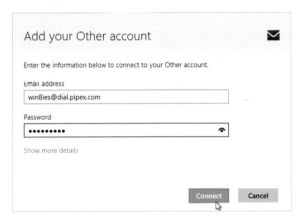

2 Mail attempts to set up the account, but if unable to
find the settings, it will ask for more information

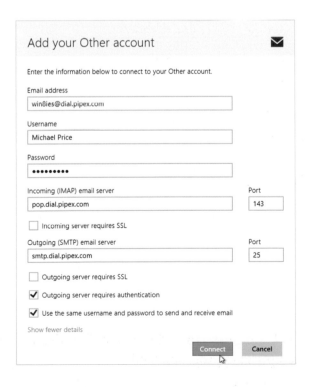

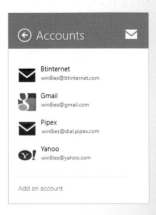

Mail App Window

These are the main components of the Mail app window:

Accounts pane   Folder pane   Reading pane   New   Respond   Delete

Active account

Current folder

Folder list

Accounts list

Folder contents   Selected message   Contents

1   Right-click an empty portion of the window to display the App bar with its additional functions

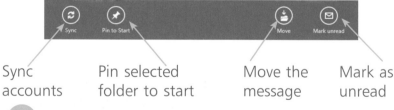

Sync accounts   Pin selected folder to start   Move the message   Mark as unread

2   Click the window to remove the App bar

The Accounts list shows unread message counts for each of the email accounts.

The Start screen tile for the Mail app shows the total new message count and features rotating extracts of the messages that are waiting to be read.

View a Message and Reply

1 Select an account, and select a message in the Folder pane and it displays in the Reading pane

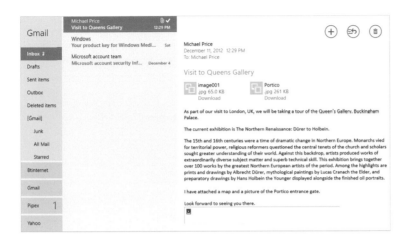

Don't forget

Touch and hold an attachment to display the menu, and select Open, Open With or Save.

2 If there are attachments, click the Download link associated with each and they will be inserted

Hot tip

You can add people from your Contacts list (see page 96) and you can also switch the account that is used to send the reply.

3 Tap Respond and then Reply, then type your reply and tap Send

4 A copy is saved in the Sent folder for the account sending the reply

Create and Send a Message

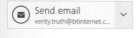
To create an email message:

1 Open Mail, select the account and its Inbox and tap the New button (or press Ctrl + N)

2 The message form is displayed for you to complete

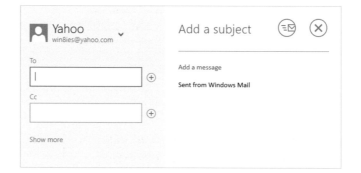

3 Begin typing the contact name in the To box, then select the contact name when it appears

4 Tap the box to add the names of more recipients

5 Tap the Cc box to add names of recipients who should be copied on this message

6 Tap Show more then tap the Bcc box to add recipients who get copied but have their names kept hidden

7 Change the priority for the message if desired, from Normal to High or Low

8 Type the Subject title, add the message text and enter your name ahead of the email signature

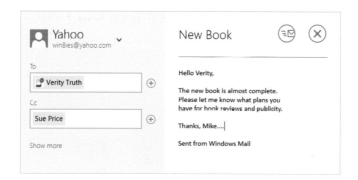

9 Right-click to display the App bar with its message handling options

10 Tap More to see additional options

11 Tap the Send button to submit the message

The message is sent to the named recipients and a copy is kept in the Sent folder for the sending account.

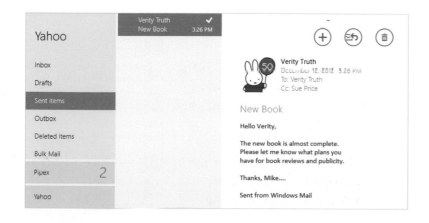

Hot tip

To view or change your email signature, open Mail Settings and select Accounts then the sending account.

Any changes that you make apply to future messages only and do not affect the current message.

93

Don't forget

The message you submit is initially transferred to the Outbox but it will be moved to the Sent folder when transfer to the Internet has completed.

People App

The People app collates and presents the details of all your contacts and makes them available to Mail, Calendar and Messaging.

1 Tap the People tile on the Start screen

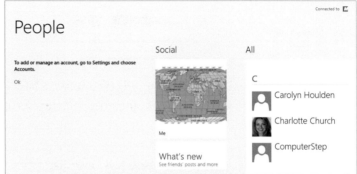

2 Display Accounts to see the accounts that are associated with the People app

3 Initially you will see just your Microsoft account

4 Tap Add an account to associate more accounts

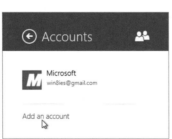

5 Choose an account type where you have an account with contacts you want to list

6 For example choose the Facebook account

7 Tap Connect to link to your Facebook account

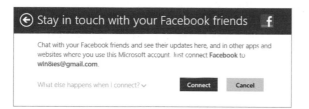

8 Enter the email account (or cell phone number) and password for your Facebook account and tap Log In

Hot tip

Each account type that you specify is added to the Connections bar.

Don't forget

To change the access settings, open the Accounts pane and select the account.

9 Select Allow to give permission for access to the various types of information listed

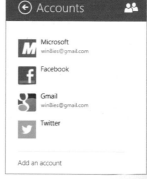

Internet Explorer opens and you'll be given the option to change settings or remove the connection.

10 Select Done when prompted and you can go to settings to add further accounts or to change the connection settings

Managing Contacts

The People app displays details of all the contacts and friends in the accounts you have defined, and keeps the lists up-to-date whenever changes occur in any of these accounts.

Hot tip

The live tile for the People app on the Start screen shows some of the images for the contacts that you have added.

1 Switch to the People app to view the latest details

2 Using Windows 8 Snap (see page 32) you can view your contacts alongside another app such as Mail

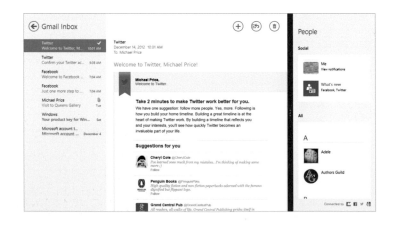

Don't forget

To show two apps side by side in this way you must have a higher resolution monitor.

3 Swipe up from the bottom edge (or right-click the app window) to display the App bar for either app

To view and change the options for the People app:

1 Display the Charms bar from inside the People app and select Settings then Options

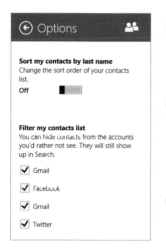

2 Click the button to sort your contacts by last name rather than first, if preferred

3 Hide the contacts from some of your accounts, to reduce the number being displayed. They still appear in searches

4 To work with a specific contact, use Search to locate and select its entry

Don't forget

To find a contact, begin typing the name and select the contact from the list of matching contacts.

5 You can send an email, send an instant message, phone the contact, map the contact's address or view more details

Hot tip

Any changes that you make to the contact's details will be shared with the originating account, the next time you Sync Mail and Contacts.

6 Right-click the details page to display the App bar

7 You can Pin to Start, mark as Favorite or Edit the contact details

97

Calendar App

The calendar that is associated with the email account used for your Microsoft account will be downloaded to your computer, and its contents will be kept in sync with the Internet copy.

1 Select the Calendar app using the associated live tile on the Start screen

2 By default, this starts up showing the calendar items for all the days of the current month

3 Display the App bar and select a view, e.g. Day

4 Select Day view and you'll see two consecutive days at once, where each day can be separately scrolled

On higher resolution monitors, for example 1920 x 1080, the Day view will show three consecutive days, each separately scrollable.

5 Select Week view and you'll see seven days (Sunday to Saturday) not separately scrollable

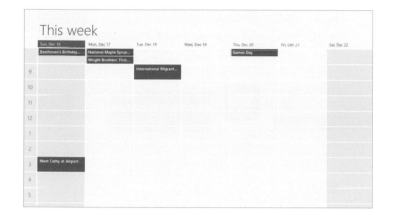

Don't forget

A sideways swipe on the screen (or one click of the mouse) will scroll the calendar one day, one week or one month, depending on the view you have set.

6 To add an entry to the calendar, tap or click the day in which the item should appear

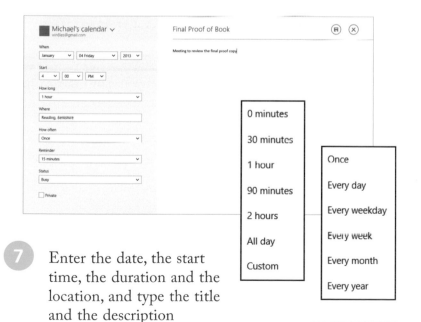

Hot tip

Specify All day for events. You can also request a reminder to be issued, up to a week before the activity or event is due to take place.

None
5 minutes
15 minutes
30 minutes
1 hour
18 hours
1 day
1 week

7 Enter the date, the start time, the duration and the location, and type the title and the description

8 Select Save and the entry will be added to your calendar

Messaging App

You can communicate instantly with friends who are online at the same time as you, with the Messaging app:

1 Select Messaging from the Start screen, and it displays a welcoming note from the Windows team

2 Swipe up from the bottom edge and select Invite from the App bar then click Add a new friend

3 Internet Explorer starts up and you can enter your friend's email address and select Next then Invite

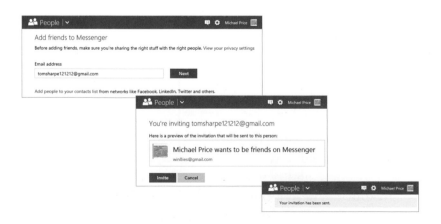

4 The invitation is sent to your friend's email account

5 Your friend will receive the invitation and can click Accept to allow communication via Messaging

Hot tip

Your contacts will need to sign in with their Microsoft account to view the details of the invitation.

View invitation

6 The invitation will be confirmed

To communicate with your friend:

1 In Messaging, click the Plus button to check which friends are online

2 Choose your friend and begin a conversation

Don't forget

You must both be online to carry out an instant messaging conversation.

Other Windows 8 Options

Don't forget

Windows Essentials (see page 76) is for Tablet PCs running Windows 8 rather than Windows RT.

If you have installed the Windows Essentials you will have alternative applications for your communications functions:

1 For instant messaging you'll select Windows Live Messenger

2 For email and Calendar, select Windows Live Mail

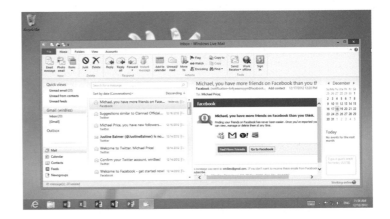

If you have installed a higher-level edition of Microsoft Office 2013 (see page 74), you have another option for electronic communications:

Hot tip

Outlook is available in the Home & Business and the Pro editions, but not in the Home & Student edition.

3 Select Outlook 2013 from the Start screen (or from the shortcut on the Taskbar)

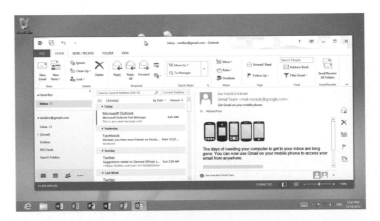

Outlook will start up on the Desktop to display your email.

7 Browsing the Internet

Windows 8 and Windows RT each have a version of Internet Explorer, and both offer two modes of operation (the full screen Windows 8 app and the standard Desktop application) so you can browse the Web in your preferred style.

Internet Connection

Don't forget

Some Tablet PCs have 3G or 4G wireless connection via the cellular network. This will require a contract with a mobile network carrier service. This can be used where there's no Wi-Fi service available, but it can be expensive, especially when used overseas.

Hot tip

When you are away from home you can connect wirelessly using the access points provided at locations such as Internet cafes, hotels and airports.

Your Tablet PC will normally connect wirelessly to the Internet via the Wi-Fi component of the DSL router on your home network. This will be set up automatically the first time that you run a new computer with Windows 8/RT pre-installed (or when you install Windows 8 on an existing computer). You'll be prompted for the network key.

You can set up the connection later, if the wireless network wasn't initially available or if you take your computer to the office or another location with a wireless network.

1 Display the Charms bar and tap Settings

2 The network icon shows wireless networks available

3 Tap the icon to display the list of networks available

4 Tap the network required, ensure that Connect automatically is ticked and tap the Connect button

5 You will be prompted for the network security key

6 Type the network security key and tap the Next button

7 Only choose to turn on sharing for home or work networks

Hot tip

If the network is used by visitors and casual users, you should choose Don't turn on sharing, even if its not a public network.

Windows will verify and connect to the network. The network will be shown as connected in the Settings and on the Network icon.

To view more details of the wireless network connection, open the Network and Sharing Center.

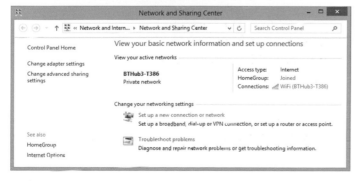

Don't forget

To open the Network and Sharing Center go to the Start screen, type network status and tap Settings, and select View network status and tasks (see page 126).

Browse Websites

You access the Internet via your browser, the default being Microsoft's Internet Explorer v10.0. There are two versions of this, for Windows 8 and Windows RT, and each has two modes – Windows 8 app and Desktop app.

1 Select the Internet Explorer tile on the Start screen to open the Windows 8 app

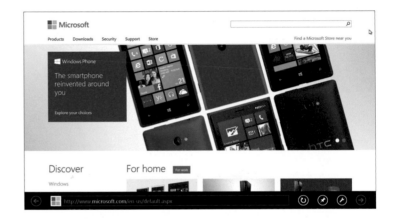

2 The app opens full screen, displaying the App bar with the website address and various buttons

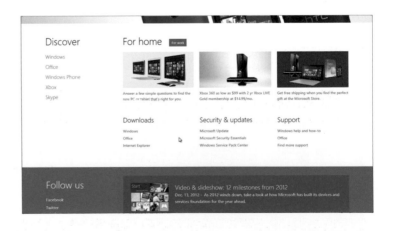

3 The App bar vanishes if you touch the screen or scroll the web page using touch, keyboard or mouse

4 Swipe up from the bottom edge or down from the top edge to redisplay the App bar, with the Tab Switcher at the top as well as the Navigation bar

Hot tip

Tap the appropriate button to display the additional functions.

Tab tools

New InPrivate tab

Close tabs

Page tools

Get app for this site

Find on page

View on the desktop

Pin to Start options

Pin to Start

Add to favorites

Tabs   Tab tools   New tab

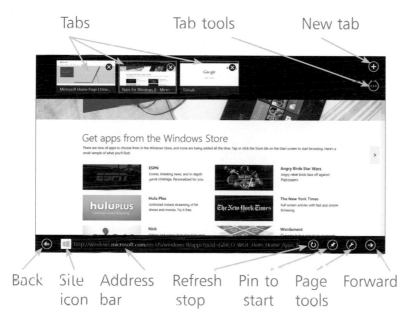

Back Site Address Refresh Pin to Page Forward
      icon bar   stop   start   tools

5 Click in the Address bar and Internet Explorer will suggest possible web pages

Don't forget

Internet Explorer keeps a history of the websites that you visit and makes suggestions based on those and on Favorites you Save and websites you Pin.

6 Begin typing until Internet Explorer identifies the required web page (or you complete the address)

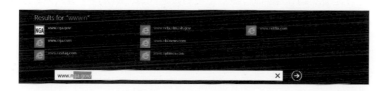

Desktop Mode

1 Select the Desktop tile from the Start menu and then the Internet Explorer icon on the Desktop Taskbar

Hot tip

Press and hold next to the Tab bar to add other bars, one at a time. Added bars are marked with a tick, Select again to remove the tick and hide the bar. You can also set Show tabs on a separate row.

2 Internet Explorer opens in a window and displays the Home page

3 Select a text or graphic hyperlink to go to that page

Address and Search bar   Tab bar   Mini toolbar

Back and Forward
Menu bar
Favorites bar
Command bar
Status bar

Web page   Slide show   Scroll bars   Video link

4 Tap the Back and Forward buttons to review pages that you have recently visited

5 Touch and hold the Back or Forward arrow to display the list of pages recently visited

6 Select the page to switch to

7 Tap the down arrow on the Address bar to Show Address bar Autocomplete

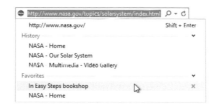

8 Internet Explorer makes suggestions based on your previous visits

Switch Internet Explorer Mode

If you are viewing a web page in the Windows 8 app mode you may find that some components do not operate as expected. You may find that Desktop mode is more compatible with that web page.

To switch modes:

1 In the Windows 8 app mode, swipe up from the bottom edge of the screen to display the App bar

2 Tap the Page Tools button and select View on the desktop

3 Review the current web page in the Desktop mode

Hot tip

The Arrows on the Title bar in Desktop mode provide the same functions as the arrows on the App bar in Windows 8 mode.

Don't forget

You can either tap an item on the web page or left-click it with the mouse. Similarly, you can either touch and hold an item or right-click it with the mouse to get the same effect.

Right-click Actions

The right-click or touch and hold action can vary depending where you click and on which mode you are in.

1 Right-click an empty part of the web page or swipe in from an edge of the screen to get the App bar

2 Right-click or touch and hold an image with no hyperlink (where the mouse pointer is an arrow) to get the Copy/Save menu

3 Right-click or touch and hold an image with a hyperlink (where the mouse pointer is a hand) and the Copy/Open Link menu is displayed

4 There's a different Copy/Open Link menu displayed when you right-click or touch and hold text with a hyperlink (also with a hand symbol)

These actions are quite unlike the results that you get with Desktop-mode Internet Explorer. To explore the differences:

5 Display the App bar, then select the Page tools to switch modes (see page 107)

...cont'd

The web page on the current tab in Windows 8 app mode is displayed in Internet Explorer in Desktop mode.

Don't forget

When you switch modes, only the active tab will be opened in Desktop mode, but you can add more tabs and switch web pages in the normal Desktop IE fashion.

6 Right-click or touch and hold various parts of the web page including images and hyperlinks and you'll see various menus, more detailed than in app mode. However, there is no App bar in Desktop mode

Plain area	Colored area	Image area	Picture hyperlink	Text hyperlink

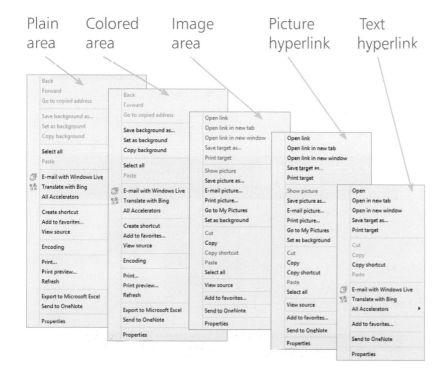

Hot tip

With hyperlinks, the right-click action menu gives options to open the link in a new window or in a new tab (see page 114).

111

App Mode Tabbed Browsing

Using tabs allows you to explore websites without losing your place in the website you are currently visiting. The appearance and effects depend on the mode you choose.

To open a web page in a new tab with Internet Explorer in the Windows 8 app mode, you can:

1 Display the App bar and select the New tab button

2 Type the address or select one of the suggested pages

3 You can also display the App bar, touch and hold (or right-click) another page and select Open in new tab

Using the keyboard, press Ctrl + T to get a new tab, or display the App bar. Type an address and press Ctrl + Enter to open it in a new tab.

4 In either case the required page opens in its own tab

5 To close an individual tab, display the Tab bar and tap or click the X on the associated thumbnail

6 To close all the tabs (except the first), display the Tab bar, tap the Tab tools button and select Close tabs

Using the On-screen Keyboard

If you have no keyboard attached to your Tablet PC, the on-screen keyboard (see page 42) will appear when you select a typing area such as the address bar.

This shows the full keyboard, but you can switch to a split keyboard intended for typing with thumbs, sometimes useful for a hand-held Tablet PC.

1 Tap the Keyboard button at the bottom right and choose the layout that you prefer to use

2 Alternatively, if you have a suitable pen you can choose the Input pad to write the text

Hot tip

Keyboard shortcut Ctrl + Alt + F4 will close all the tabs except the current tab, just as it does in the Desktop version. You don't have to display the Tab bar, though it does let you see the action.

Don't forget

The full on-screen keyboard will take up less of the screen area if you rotate your Tablet PC into the Portrait orientation (see page 169).

Desktop Tabbed Browsing

With Internet Explorer in Desktop mode, tabs are on the Tab bar rather than the App bar, but offer similar features.

To open a web page in a new tab:

Hot tip

The New Tab button gives you a blank tab where you can enter a URL on the address bar, or redisplay your previously-viewed web pages.

1 Tap or click the New Tab button or press Ctrl + T and the new tab is added as the current tab

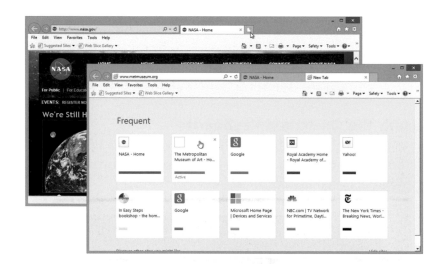

Don't forget

You can use the on-screen keyboard to type the address, but you'll need to tap the Keyboard button on the Taskbar to show the keyboard.

2 Type the web page address in the address bar (or select from the suggestions) and press Enter

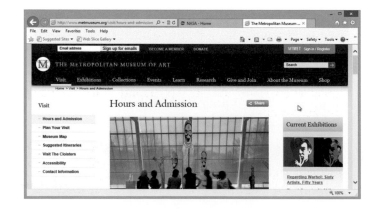

3 The new tab displays the required web page, with the previous web page still available on the other tab

4   Touch and hold or right-click a hyperlink on the current web page (see page 111) and select Show Link in New Tab, or press Ctrl + Click

5   The new tab is added but the original tab remains displayed. Select the new tab to view the new page

As you add tabs the Tab bar becomes full. Scroll buttons are added when there are too many tabs to fit on at one time.

6   Hold the mouse pointer over a tab to see the full title of the web page that it displays

7   Tap the Internet Explorer icon on the Taskbar (or hover the mouse over it) to display thumbnails of all the active tabs

8   Select the thumbnail for the web page that you want to make the current tab

Hot tip

If you press Ctrl + Shift + Click to select a hyperlink, it will display immediately in the new tab.

Don't forget

If there are too many tab thumbnails to fit across the screen, the tabs will be shown as a list of web page titles, from which you can choose the one you want to display.

Close Tabs in Desktop

Hot tip

If you have a wheel mouse, click a tab on the tab row with the wheel to close that tab. You could also tap or click the icon on the Taskbar and click the thumbnail with the wheel to close the tab.

1 To close the current tab, tap or click the X on the tab (or press Ctrl + W or press Alt + F4)

2 To close all of the tabs except for the current tab, you'd press Ctrl + Alt + F4

3 To close the Internet Explorer session, tap or click the X on the window title bar, press Alt + F4, or touch and hold (or right-click) the title bar and select Close

4 You could also touch and hold (or right-click) the taskbar icon and select Close window from the Jump list

5 When you Close the session with more than one tab open, you are prompted to select Close all tabs or Close current tab

The next time you start Internet Explorer in Desktop mode, you can restore all the previously-open tabs.

6 Open a new tab (see page 114) and select Reopen last browsing session

Don't forget

This is useful for continuing work in progress, but if you will need the same set of web pages at a later date, save them as a group favorite.

Add to Favorites

When you find a web page that you know you'll want to visit in the future, save it as a Favorite. In Desktop mode:

1 Display the web page, tap the Favorites button and then tap Add to Favorites

Hot tip

To make your favorites easier to identify, you can change the name, select a different folder from the list, or create a new folder.

2 Tap Add to put the named entry in the main folder

3 To save the open tabs as a set, tap the down-arrow and select Add Current Tabs to Favorites

4 Provide a Folder Name for the set of tabs and tap Add

Favorites Center

To make use of the entries saved in your Favorites list:

5 Tap the Favorites button, then select the whole tab group, a web page from within the group, or a web page saved individually

Hot tip

Tap the arrow button to pin the Favorites Center to the window so that you can quickly view each of the entries in turn.

Pin Favorites

Internet Explorer can also add web pages to the list of Favorites when in the App mode. To add a web page:

1 Display the web page and the App bar and select the Pin button, then tap Add to favorites

2 Whenever you touch the address bar to enter a web address, Favorites are listed, alongside Frequent sites

3 To see the latest Favorites, you must scroll to the end

4 Alternatively, you can select Pin to Start and accept or amend the suggested website title, then tap Pin to Start, and your Pinned websites will appear first in the list of suggested websites

Zoom Web Page

You may find some web pages difficult to read, especially if you have your monitor set for high resolution. The Zoom feature provides an effective solution to this problem.

Don't forget

On your Tablet PC or on a touchscreen you can use the Pinch and Stretch gestures (see page 27) to zoom out and zoom in.

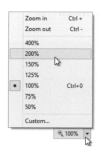

① Tap the arrow next to the Zoom button on the Status bar and choose a level, e.g. 200%

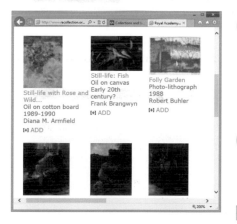

② Tap the Zoom button to return to the 100% level

③ Tap Zoom again to cycle through levels 100%, 125%, 150%

119

Hot tip

Press Ctrl+ to Zoom in, 25% more at a time, press Ctrl- to Zoom out, 25% less each time and press Ctrl+0 to return to the 100% level.

④ Select Custom from the menu to specify a zoom factor (10-1000%). Tap an arrow to raise or lower the value or type a new number

Values below 100% are useful when you want to overview a large web page, to get an idea of the overall shape and style of the contents. You can then zoom in to read the detail.

...cont'd

Select Internet Options and adjust Zoom slider where you can set a value between 50% and 400% as the default. This only affects the Windows 8 Internet Explorer app.

In the App mode, Internet Explorer app accepts the same keyboard shortcuts, but there is no Zoom menu or button.

1. With full screen display always in effect, some web pages may not make full use of the display area

2. Press Ctrl+ four times to apply a zoom factor of 200% and the web page fills the width of the screen

Swipe the screen up or down or across to view other parts. Press Ctrl + 0 to return to the 100% zoom level.

8 Networking

If you have other PCs as well as your Tablet PC, you can create and join networks, and share information with your HomeGroup of users on your private network. When you travel with your PC, you can join public networks at locations such as coffee shops and hotels.

Create a Network

A network consists of several separate devices that operate independently but are connected via wire or radio waves, allowing them to share information. The starting point for your network is your computer and the router that links to the Internet for email and browsing. You can add other computers and other devices, to share the Internet access and to exchange information with one another.

Hot tip

This is based on the network map feature in Windows 7. There's no map feature in Windows 8, but the same types of connections are supported.

122

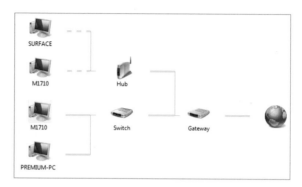

For computers that are based on Windows 8 (or Windows 7), a HomeGroup can be created to make it easier to share data.

To make the connections, you use:

- Ethernet twisted-pair cables, for the wired portion
- A Switch to manage the wired network connections
- A wireless Hub to mange the wireless connections
- A Router to enable the connection with the Internet
- An Adapter for each computer (wired or wireless)

The switch, hub and router functions may be included as separate devices, or may be incorporated in one multi-function device.

The wired or wireless adapters may be built in to the computers, or may be added, for example as USB devices.

Don't forget

Tablet PCs normally feature built-in wireless adapters. Some models also incorporate mobile broadband, so they can connect to the Internet without requiring a router.

Wired Connection

1 Install the network adapter if needed and start Windows, with no network connection

2 Display the Charms bar and tap Settings. The Network icon shows Unavailable

3 Tap the icon to confirm No connections available

Don't forget

Windows automatically detects the network and sets up the connection, if there is a cable in place when you start up. Leaving the cable unattached allows you to see the stages involved.

4 Add a cable between the adapter and the switch and the computer is connected to the Network

5 Tap the Network icon, touch and hold or right-click the Network and tap Turn sharing on or off

Hot tip

The default name for a wired network is simply the word "Network" itself.

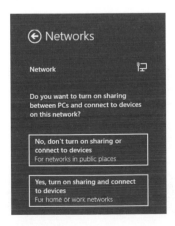

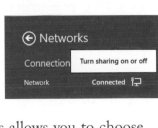

This allows you to choose the level of sharing, which will be determined by the type of network that you are connecting with (see page 124).

Network Type

Don't forget

To see the details of the network connection, you can open the Network and Sharing center (see page 126).

1 Choose Yes, turn on sharing and connect to devices, for networks at home or at work

This gives a **Private network** for home or work networks or for known and trusted environments. The computer can create or join a HomeGroup and share data with others.

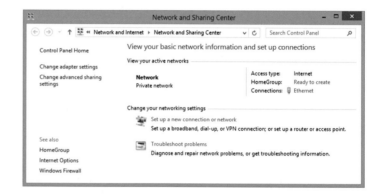

2 Choose No, don't turn on sharing or connect to devices, for networks that are in public places

This gives a **Public network** for guest use or for networks in coffee shops, hotels or airports. HomeGroup is not available.

Don't forget

You can allow guest or casual users to join your network with a Public connection, to restrict their access to your system and data.

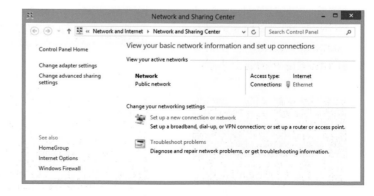

Wireless Connection

To set up the connection, if your Tablet PC has a wireless adapter:

1 Display the Charms bar and tap Settings

2 The Network icon tells you what networks are Available

3 Tap the icon to display the connections and tap your main wireless network

4 Tap the box to Connect automatically and then tap Connect

5 Type the network security key and tap Next

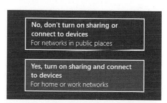

6 Choose your sharing option (see page 123), e.g. Yes, turn on sharing

7 The network is shown as connected and the name from the wireless hub

Beware

Your system will detect all wireless networks in the vicinity, so make sure you select the correct entry.

Don't forget

Your computer will be Ready to create a new HomeGroup, or Available to join an existing HomeGroup (see page 132).

Access type:	Internet
HomeGroup:	Ready to create
Connections:	Wi-Fi (BTHub3-T386)

Access type:	Internet
HomeGroup:	Available to join
Connections:	Wi-Fi (BTHub3-T386)

Network and Sharing Center

Hot tip

Alternatively, open the Control Panel and select View network status and tasks.

Another option is to touch and hold (or right-click) the Network icon on the Taskbar and select Open Network and Sharing Center.

1 Display Search Settings, type network center and select the entry for Network and Sharing Center

2 View the basic information for your networks, such as network type, connections and HomeGroup status

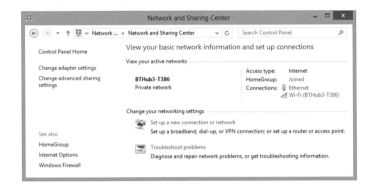

3 Click Change advanced sharing settings, to review the options for Private and for Public networks

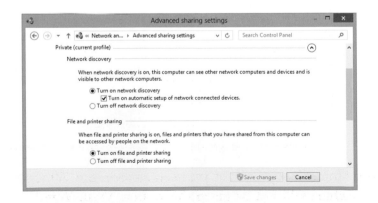

Hot tip

Private networks will have Network discovery and File and printer sharing turned on. For Public networks, these will be turned off.

Add Windows RT Computer

If your Tablet PC is running Windows RT rather than Windows 8, you set up the network connection in the same manner. For example, with a wireless connection:

1 Display the Charms bar and select Settings

2 Tap the Network icon and proceed to select your wireless network, provide the network security key, and turn on sharing

3 The network is assigned a name and shown as connected

Open the Network and Sharing Center to view the connection details. If the HomeGroup has already been created, the Windows RT finds it Available to join.

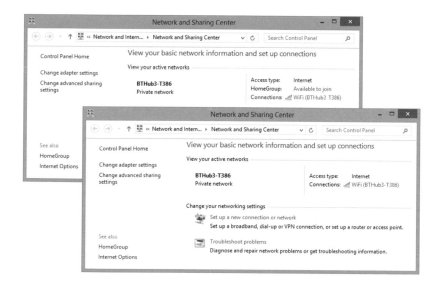

If the HomeGroup has not yet been created, the Windows RT machine will not be given this option. With Windows RT you can join but not create a HomeGroup.

Hot tip

Turning on sharing will establish a Private network on which the HomeGroup will be supported.

127

Don't forget

Tablet PCs that run Windows RT can join a HomeGroup and share the data on other computers, but they cannot share their own data on the network. If there's no existing HomeGroup, they can't create one.

HomeGroup

There's no homegroup on this network
You can't create your own homegroup with this PC, but you can join a homegroup created by someone else.

Create HomeGroup

Don't forget

If a HomeGroup has already been created on the network, you get the option to join that HomeGroup (see page 132).

When you set up the connection for a Windows 8 computer on a Private network you can create a HomeGroup for it, assuming that one has not yet been established.

One way to do this is from the PC Settings.

 Display the Charms bar, tap Settings and select Change PC Settings

 Select HomeGroup to display the current status

Beware

If there's already a HomeGroup on your network but its computers are hibernating or powered off, any new computer might think there is no HomeGroup. You should start up one of the computers before selecting the HomeGroup entry.

 Tap Create and Windows sets up the HomeGroup and password, and lists your resources for sharing

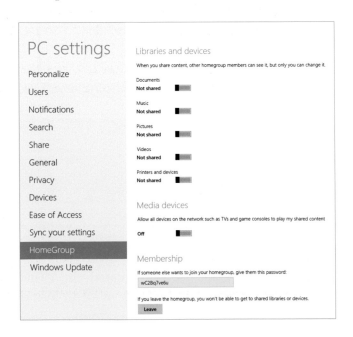

4 Tap the switch for Documents, Music, Pictures, Videos or Printers and devices, to share that resource

Hot tip

You can limit the file types that are shared. Note that other computers can access but not change the shared data.

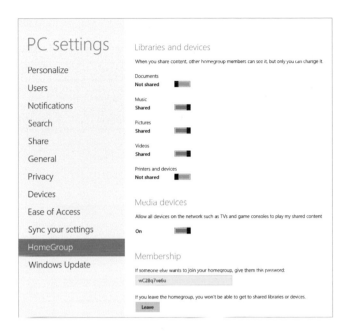

5 Tap the switch for Media Devices to allow TVs and games consoles etc. to access the shared content

6 The Network and Sharing Center changes the HomeGroup status from Ready to create, to Joined

Don't forget

The password is a random combination of lower case, upper case and numbers. However, you can change the password to something more easily remembered, if you wish.

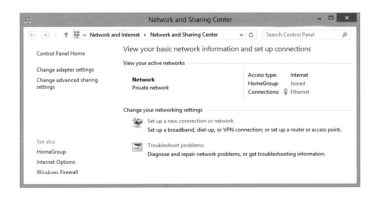

Create from Network Center

1 With a private network, open the Network and Sharing Center and tap Ready to create

2 Tap the button Create a homegroup to start sharing

3 Amend the sharing options if desired then tap Next to set up the HomeGoup

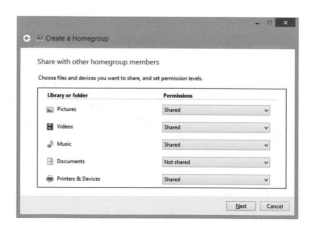

4 Windows automatically generates a secure password for the HomeGroup that you can give to others

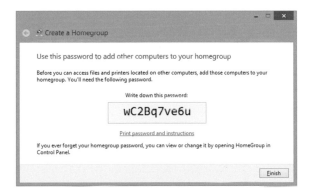

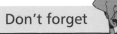
Don't forget

The password will be used for any other computer on the network that is meant to join the HomeGroup.

5 Make a note of the new password and tap Finish, and the HomeGroup settings are displayed

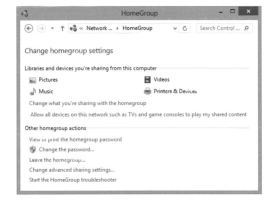

Hot tip

To revisit HomeGroup settings, open the Network and Sharing Center and select HomeGroup from the list on the left.

6 From the HomeGroup Settings screen you can:
- Change what you're sharing with the homegroup
- Allow access by all devices on this network
- View or print the homegroup password
- Change the password to a more memorable value

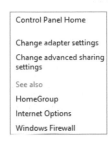
Control Panel Home

Change adapter settings
Change advanced sharing settings

See also

HomeGroup
Internet Options
Windows Firewall

7 Tap the Back arrow to return to the Network and Sharing Center, or tap the Close button

Join the HomeGroup

Don't forget

When you add a computer to a private network, Windows will detect an available HomeGroup.

1 Display the Charms bar, select Settings and Change PC Settings then tap HomeGroup

2 Type the HomeGroup password and tap Join

Hot tip

Initially, none of the libraries is shown as shared, but you can select those that you want to make available to other members of the HomeGroup.

3 Tap the switches to turn sharing on or off for the individual libraries and devices

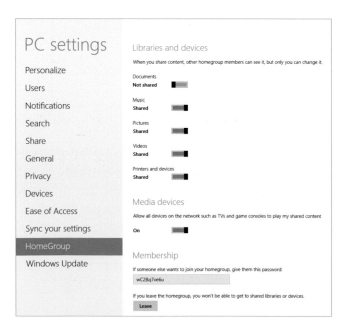

1 Alternatively, open the Network and Sharing Center and tap Available to join now then tap Join now

Access type:	Internet
HomeGroup:	Available to join
Connections:	WiFi (BTHub3-T386)

2 Choose the items you want to share and click Next

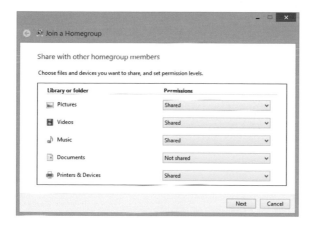

3 Type the HomeGroup password and click Next

133

Join with Windows RT

When you join a HomeGroup from a computer running Windows RT, you cannot share your own data, though you can access data shared by others. This applies whichever way you join the HomeGroup.

1 Display the HomeGroup in PC Settings, then type the HomeGroup password and tap Join

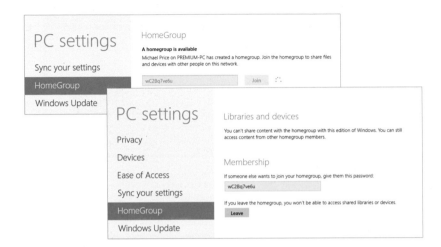

You can't share your libraries and devices, but you can access the items shared by other members of the HomeGroup.

2 Alternatively, select Available to Join in the Network and Sharing Center, where you are reminded you can't create a HomeGroup or share files and devices

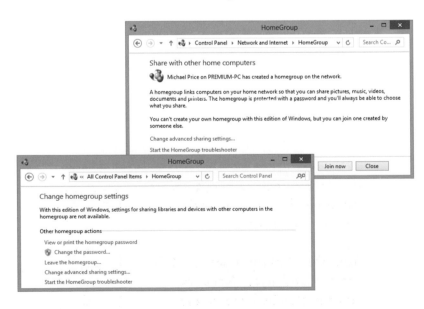

Hot tip

Settings for sharing libraries and devices are not available, but you can apply other HomeGroup actions such as View, Print or Change the password.

View Devices

You can find a list of all the computers and other devices that are connected and active on your network.

1 Display the Charms bar, select Search then select Settings, then type "view devices" and select from the results View devices and printers

Don't forget

You can also press WinKey + W to display Search with Settings already selected and ready for you to enter search text.

2 The Control Panel, Hardware and Sound, Devices and Printers category is displayed showing all devices

Don't forget

Alternatively, you can display Search Settings, type view devices as above, and select View network computers and devices.

3 The devices include hub, Internet connected TV, shared media libraries and printers

4 From the Desktop, open the File Explorer and select Networks to view the attached computers

...cont'd

A computer that is powered off or in sleep mode will have its entries removed. When the computer is activated its entries are added.

5 File Explorer displays the computers and devices that are currently active on the network

6 Select HomeGroup and expand the entries to see the media devices that are available for sharing

7 This shows items from computers that have joined and shared libraries. This excludes Windows RT PCs

8 File Explorer shows similar results for Network and HomeGroup on a Windows RT PC

You will also find Devices and Printers in the Hardware and Sound category in the Control Panel.

9 You can also View devices and printers on the Windows RT PC, using Search Settings (see page 135)

Travel with the Tablet PC

The networking interface makes it easier to connect while you are traveling and when you arrive at your destination.

If you are flying, you may be allowed to use your Tablet PC while in the air, but there are things look out for, such as:

- Fully charge the battery before leaving – you are unlikely to be able to recharge during the flight

- Make sure you pack the power charger

- Carry proof of ownership (Customs might want it)

- Turn on Airplane mode before boarding the plane

Hot tip

You can also open the Charms bar, select Settings and tap the Network icon to find the switch that turns Flight mode on or off.

1   Display Charms bar, Settings and open PC Settings

PC settings

	Flight mode
Privacy	Turn this on to stop wireless communication
	Off
Devices	
	Wireless devices
Wireless	
	WiFi
	On
Ease of Access	Bluetooth
Sync your settings	On

2   Select Wireless and tap the Flight mode On button

Don't forget

Turn Flight mode On and you will turn off all wireless devices, including Wi-Fi and Bluetooth.

PC settings

	Flight mode
Privacy	Turn this on to stop wireless communication
	On
Devices	
	Wireless devices
Wireless	
	WiFi
	Off
Ease of Access	Bluetooth
Sync your settings	Off

- Be sure to power off your Tablet PC during takeoff and landing, and check that use during flight is permitted

...cont'd

When you arrive at your destination:

1. Display Charms bar, Settings and tap the Network icon and select the wireless network at your location

2. Tap Connect, choose to log in via the web browser and type the username and password provided

3. Accept terms and tap Login

4. Switch to the website you want to access

9 Users and Data

Share your Tablet PC with others, giving them their own libraries and settings, and allowing the appropriate level of access for children and guests. Keep the file history so your data is safe and learn how to restore your system.

New User Account

1 Open PC Settings (see page 128) and select Users, then tap the button to Add a user

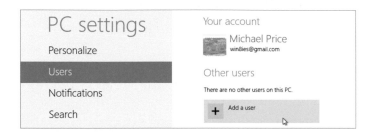

2 Type an email address for the new user, preferably one that's associated with a Microsoft account

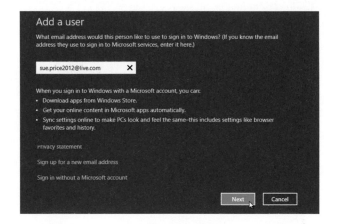

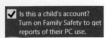
3 Tap Next and follow the prompts to create and/or access the Microsoft account

4 The new user is defined to the system, ready to sign on for the first time

You can allow a new user to sign on while you are still logged on to the PC.

5 From the Start screen, tap the username or picture and select the new user account

6 Alternatively, select Lock, tap the arrow next to the Last user signed on and select the account

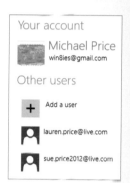

7 If you Sign out or Shut down, you can restart and select the required account from the Logon screen

8 In each case, the sign on screen for the selected user account will be displayed ready for setup

First Sign-on

1 Enter the password for the new account and tap the arrow (or press Enter on the keyboard)

2 Windows presents a brief tutorial while it creates the user libraries and folders and installs the apps

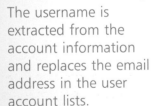
3 When initialization completes, the Start screen will be displayed, showing the new user account

Change Account Type

1 From Control Panel, User Accounts and Family Safety tap Change account type

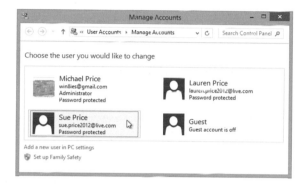

2 Tap one of the new accounts

3 Tap Change the account type and you'll see that it has been defined as Standard

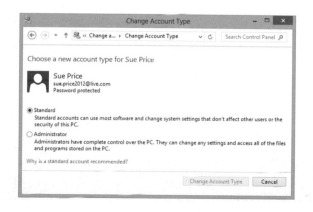

143

Don't forget

This displays details of the accounts on your computer. Note that the first account created when the system was originally set up has been defined as Administrator.

Hot tip

Note that you cannot create new accounts from within the Control Panel, but must select the link to Add a new user in PC Settings.

Hot tip

Standard user accounts are recommended for every user, even the administrator, to minimize the risk of unintended changes. Windows will ask for the administrator password, when that level is needed.

Guest Account

Windows provides a Guest account for casual use, by visitors for example. By default this is turned off. To enable it:

1 Select Change account type from Control Panel and tap on the entry for the Guest account

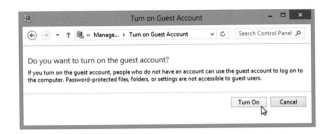

2 Tap the button to Turn On the Guest account

3 The Guest account is enabled as Local (without the ability to access the Windows Store and install apps)

4 Tap the Guest account entry to view change options

5 You find the only option offered is to turn off the Guest account

Set Up Family Safety

To set up Family Safety for an account on the computer:

1 Select Set up Family Safety from Control Panel, User Accounts and Family Safety

2 Select an account with Family Safety turned on

3 Check that Activity Reporting is turned on and review access settings and restrictions being applied

4 View reports and summaries for user activities including PC time and apps and games used

Don't forget

Family Safety provides parental controls in Windows 8, to filter websites, set time limits on computer use, monitor and restrict apps from the Windows Store and send activity reports via email to parents.

Hot tip

You can turn on Family Safety for an account not currently monitored, or turn off Family Safety for an account that is being monitored.

Don't forget

You will find a more comprehensive activity report on the Family Safety website.

Managing Data

In Windows 8, data resources are primarily managed by the apps associated with the type of data, such as Photos, to find and view pictures, or Music to locate and play songs.

1. Tap the Music tile on the Start screen

2. The Music app opens and gives access to music on your computer and at the Xbox music store

3. Use the app to create playlists, play music by specific artists or explore the contents of your music library

4. To locate particular items, use Search from the Charms bar and enter appropriate keywords

5 To search on your computer only, select the Files category

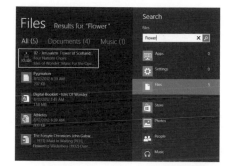

6 This looks in all libraries and, in this case, finds relevant entries in Music and Documents

You can also search in the libraries on your computer using File Explorer on the Desktop.

7 Tap the Desktop tile on the Start screen and the File Explorer icon on the Taskbar

Hot tip

To display the libraries when there's a folder window open, tap the Libraries entry in the Navigation pane on the left.

8 Select the Search box and type the keywords

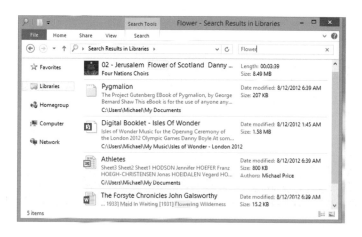

Don't forget

If you open a specific library (or drive or folder), the Search will be directed at that part of your disc storage.

Libraries

The Libraries in Windows 8 provide a place where you can manage your documents, music, pictures and other files. There are four default libraries – Documents, Music, Pictures and Videos, which give you a combined view of the relevant folders for the current user and the Public folders.

To examine the components of a library:

1 Open File Explorer from the Taskbar icon and double-tap one of the libraries, Music for example

2 As indicated on the Status bar, the library includes two locations – My Music and Public Music

3 Tap the Library name in the Navigation pane and tap the white triangle (▷) to expand the list (or the black triangle (◢) to collapse the list)

Items in the Public Music folder are available to all users on the computer. Items in My Music are private to the specific user, unless joined to the HomeGroup (see page 132).

see page 132

Don't forget

To change the view in which the library contents are displayed, tap View and select an option from Layout, for example Large icons which can be useful for Tablet PCs.

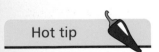

Hot tip

The other libraries will similarly include two locations, one available to all users and one that can be kept private if desired.

To see how these folders are stored on your hard drive:

1 Select Computer in the Navigation pane and then select the System drive (C:) and double-tap Users

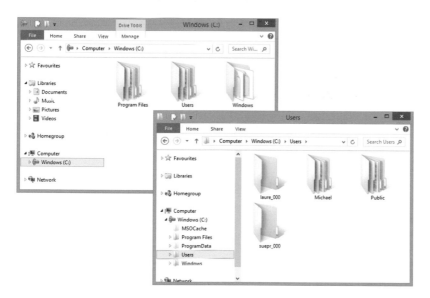

2 Double-tap and open the current user folder, in this case Michael, and then open a library, e.g. Music

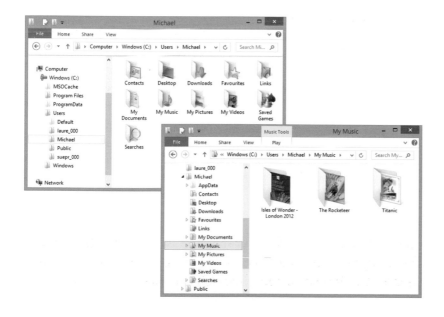

Don't forget

There's a folder for each user defined on the system, plus the Public folder.

Don't forget

Each User folder has folders for Contacts, Downloads, Favorites, Links, Saved Games and Searches, plus folders for the four libraries: Documents, Music, Pictures and Videos libraries. The Public folder has Downloads plus the four libraries.

File History

Don't forget

You can protect the files in your personal libraries using the File History feature. This allows you to recover files that are damaged or accidentally deleted or modified.

Hot tip

In this case, the Tablet PC uses a removable micro SD drive. You can tap Select drive to find an alternative removable drive, and Add network location to select a folder on another computer on the network.

Available drives
- Removable Disk (D:)
- INTENSO (E:)
- \\Premium-pc\c\SurfaceBackup

To enable File History:

 Select File History from the Control Panel, or open Search Settings. Type file history and tap the matching item

 File History identifies an external or network drive to use for backup. Tap Turn on to accept the drive

3 An initial backup of your files is taken and regular backups of changes are carried out thereafter

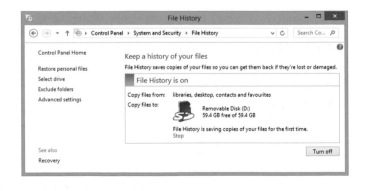

4 Tap Advanced settings to change the frequency of backups and to specify a time limit for the backups

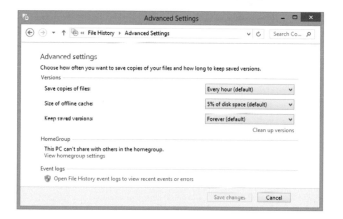

By default, backup copies will be created every hour and will be kept forever (or until the available space has been used up, when older backups will be released).

5 Select a file in File Explorer and tap Home, History on the ribbon to see all its backups displayed in Player style

Don't forget

You can choose files from any of the backups, to restore a file that has been deleted or to revert a file to a previous version.

6 Select Restore personal files to browse the backups stored on the File History drive

System Restore

Problems may arise when you install new software or a new device. If uninstalling does not correct the situation, you can return the system files to their values prior to the changes.

1 From the Charms bar tap search, type "recovery", tap Settings and select the Recovery option

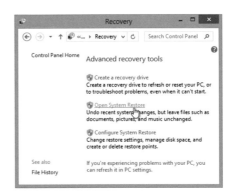

2 Select Open System Restore then select Next

3 Choose the appropriate Restore point and tap Next

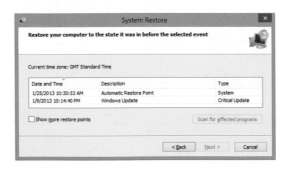

4 Click Finish to confirm your selected restore point

5 Select Yes to confirm the System Restore

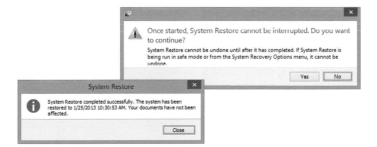

6 Your computer will be restarted and the requested System Restore Point will be applied

7 You can still run System Restore to undo the restore

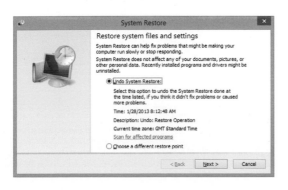

Don't forget

Once started, System Restore cannot be interrupted, though it can be undone (unless run from Safe Mode or the System Recovery Options menu).

Hot tip

If the selected restore point does not resolve your problems, you can undo the restore or try a different restore point.

System Recovery Options

There are more advanced tools available to help recovery from problem situations.

1 Open PC Settings, select General and then tap Restart now in the Advanced Startup section

2 Select the Troubleshoot option, and from that screen select the Advanced options

3 Advanced options include System Restore, System Image Recovery and Automatic Repair

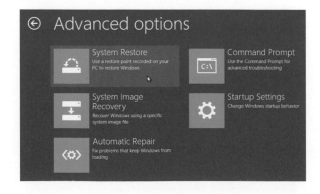

10 Manage your Tablet PC

Make your Tablet PC look and feel the way you want, using the tools provided to adjust its appearance and operation. Manage your sign on options, and make your preferred settings available on other computers that you sign on to using the same Microsoft account.

Personalization

Windows 8 offers two sets of facilities for customizing your PC setup: in the Windows 8 app environment using PC Settings and on the Desktop using the Control Panel (see page 166). If you sign on with a Microsoft account, you can take the changes with you when you sign on at other computers.

To change using PC Settings:

1   Display the Charms bar and tap Settings (or press WinKey + I) to display the Settings pane

2   Tap the link to Change PC Settings

3   The PC Settings screen is displayed, with the Personalize category selected

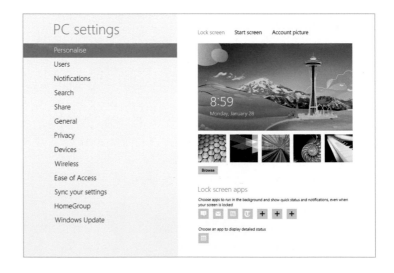

4   From this screen you can change the setup and appearance of the Lock screen, the Start screen and your Account picture

Personalize Lock Screen

The Lock screen appears when you start your Windows 8 computer or resume from Sleep. To customize this screen:

1 In PC Settings, Personalize, tap the Lock screen tab

Don't forget

When you select a different Lock screen picture, it changes the Lock screen image in any other computer where you sign in with the same Microsoft account.

2 Tap one of the six supplied pictures to make it the current background image

3 Tap Browse to select an image from your Pictures library or another folder on your hard disk

4 Scroll down the Lock screen pane to choose Windows 8 Apps to display notifications and updates on the Lock screen

Hot tip

You can use any image file type, including GIF, JPEG, PNG and TIFF. The image will be adjusted as necessary.

Don't forget

You can choose seven Windows 8 apps in total to provide simple Quick Status updates, and just a single app to provide more detailed updates.

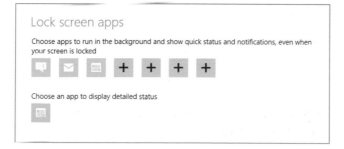

...cont'd

5 Tap the Add icon to choose an app from the list, and tap an existing App icon and choose a different app or tap Don't show quick status here to remove the app

6 Similarly, you can choose or change the single app that will display detailed status or select the option Don't show detailed status on the Lock screen to remove an app

You can Lock your Tablet PC to review the changes without having to wait until the next time you log on to the system. To do this:

1 On the Start screen tap the active user name or picture

2 Select Lock to display the Lock screen

Network status Mail waiting Date and time Meeting notice

Start Screen

1 In PC Settings, Personalize, tap the Start screen tab

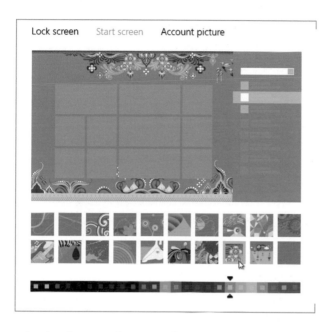

Choose the background image for your Start screen:

2 Select one of the 20 panels supplied

3 Drag the slider to choose a different foreground/ background color set from the 25 shown

4 View the effects on the Start screen illustration which gets updated instantly

5 Press the Windows button (WinKey) to toggle between Settings and Start screen, to see the effects

Like other Personalization effects, this change is shared with other computers that you sign on to with the same Microsoft account. Other users on the computer can have their own personalization settings that travel with them when they sign on to other machines. Their settings are not affected by your choices.

Don't forget

The Color set will be used in all Windows 8 apps, as well as the Start screen. The image panel is used only for the Start screen.

Don't forget

You cannot choose your own images for the Start screen, as you can with the Lock screen and the Desktop, unless you install a third-party product such as Decor8.

Account Picture

You can specify a photo or image to appear alongside your username on the Start screen.

1 In PC Settings tap Personalize and select the Account picture tab

2 Click the Browse button to select an existing image from your Pictures library or another folder on your hard disk

3 Alternatively, if your computer has a webcam or built-in camera, select Camera to take a picture

4 You can take a still photo or a video, but the video is limited to five seconds

5 Press the Windows button to toggle between the Settings screen and the Start screen, to see the results

6 The picture will also be displayed with your username on the Sign on screen ready for password entry

If you are signed on with a Microsoft account, the selected image will be displayed on the Start screen of any Windows 8 computer where you sign on with that account.

Sync your Settings

When you sign on using a Microsoft account, Windows will sync your settings on all PCs you use. To view the details:

1 Open PC Settings and select Sync your settings

Hot tip

If you'd like to make a setting specific to the particular machine, tap the switch for that setting to turn it off. This setting will be unaffected on any other machines.

2 You may see a note saying Your passwords won't sync until you trust this PC

> **Passwords**
> Your passwords won't sync until you trust this PC.
> Trust this PC

3 Tap Trust this PC to go to the Live.com website and click Confirm to make the current PC trusted

> Win8
> Confirm | Delete

Don't forget

You normally complete security verification when you sign on to the PC for the first time (see page 24). It's only if you skipped that step that you get a PC Settings prompt to Trust this PC.

Picture Password

Don't forget

The picture password consists of three gestures, applied in sequence at specific locations. You can choose one or other of three types of gesture – a circle, a straight line or a screen tap.

1 In PC Settings, select Users and then Create a picture password

2 Enter your current password to confirm and click OK

3 Note the instructions for drawing on the screen to add gestures to your picture

4 Tap Choose picture then select the picture from your hard disk folders and click Open

Hot tip

If you have trouble repeating your initial selection, click Try again to see prompts, or Start over to enter a new set of gestures.

5 Follow the prompts to position the picture and tap Use this picture (or tap Choose new picture), then draw the three gestures and confirm your three gestures

6   When you've successfully confirmed and your picture password is set up, click Finish

Don't forget

The selected gestures – a circle, a line and a tap – are shown here as an illustration, but such indicators will not normally appear on the display except when you are having problems during the initial definition.

The next time the Lock screen appears and you sign on, you'll be able to use your picture password.

163

Don't forget

You'd normally use picture passwords with a touchscreen, but you can use the mouse to draw and tap.

You can still use your password for signing on.

1   Click Switch to password

2   Type your password and press Enter to sign on

Tap the Sign-in options link to choose between the methods

PIN Code

1 In PC Settings, tap Users and then tap Create a PIN

2 Enter your current password to confirm and tap OK

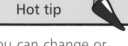
3 Enter the PIN code digits using the touch keypad or an attached keyboard

4 Enter the PIN code a second time to confirm the values

5 Select Finish when the values are entered

When you next sign on, you'll be asked to provide the PIN, by touch or by keyboard, with no need to press Enter.

Click Sign-in options to switch between the Picture password, the PIN code and your Microsoft account password.

Ease of Access

PC Settings also allows you to set up Ease of Access options on your computer, to improve usability.

1 In PC Settings, select the Ease of Access category

2 Click the appropriate button to turn On or Off

High contrast

Make everything on your screen bigger (if supported for your particular display)

Don't forget

You can adjust the size of text and/or graphics on your system using the Display settings (see page 168).

165

3 Pick the action for the WinKey + Volume Up combination. The default is Narrator

Nothing
Magnifier
Narrator
On-Screen Keyboard

4 Choose the duration for which notifications will display. The default is five seconds, but you can set a time of up to five minutes

5 seconds
7 seconds
15 seconds
30 seconds
1 minute
5 minutes

Don't forget

On the Microsoft Surface Tablet PCs, the Windows button (WinKey)+ Volume Down combination is used to save screenshots to a folder in the Pictures library.

5 You can also increase the cursor thickness from the default of one pixel width to any value up to 20 pixels width

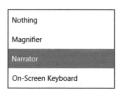

There are more comprehensive Ease of Access functions provided in the Control Panel (see page 170) in the Ease of Access category.

Open Control Panel

For more comprehensive options for customizing your system, use the Control Panel. Ways to open this include:

1 Select Search from the Charms bar and start typing control. Tap the Control Panel entry that appears

2 From the Desktop with Show desktop icons enabled, double-tap the Control Panel icon

3 From File Explorer, select Computer, tap the Computer tab and select Open Control Panel

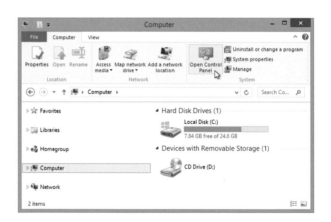

4 From the Desktop, display the Charms bar, tap Settings and select the Control Panel entry

The Control Panel entry does not appear on the Settings when the Charms bar has been opened from the Start screen or from any other app than the Desktop.

Personalize via Control Panel

When the Control Panel opens, you see the categories as displayed in previous versions of Windows. To personalize:

1. Select the Appearance and Personalization option

2. Select Personalization to adjust the Desktop

3. Choose a theme or change individual characteristics

Don't forget

Control Panel is a Desktop app and so will open as a window on the Desktop.

Hot tip

You can also display Personalization by selecting Personalize from the Desktop dropdown menu (see page 168).

Don't forget

To choose which system icons appear on the Desktop, select Change desktop icons and select or clear the boxes for the icons.

Display Settings

Don't forget

Display options other than resolution affect the PC in Desktop mode only and do not affect Start screen and Windows 8 apps.

1 Select Display from Control Panel, Appearance and Personalization

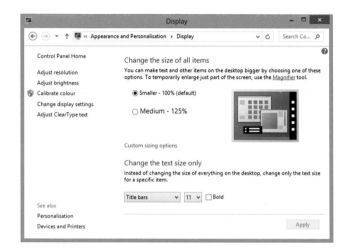

2 Change the size of text and other items, or select a function such as Adjust resolution

Hot tip

You can also select Screen resolution from the Desktop dropdown menu, to switch to this panel.

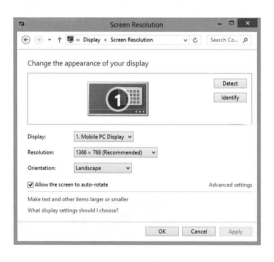

3 Here you can choose the orientation, disable auto-rotation or reset the resolution for your screen

4 Tap the down arrow next to Resolution

5 Drag the slider to select a new resolution and tap Apply

| OK | Cancel | Apply |

The higher the resolution, the more you can fit on the screen, but the smaller the text and images will then appear.

6 Tap the arrow next to Orientation to select Landscape or Portrait, making them Flipped if desired

7 After any change, you are asked to confirm you want to keep the changes, or they'll automatically revert

If you can attach a second display (or a projector) to your Tablet PC, you can control how it will be used.

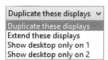

More Ease of Access

1   From Control Panel select the Ease of Access category

2   You can set up speech recognition with a microphone, or go to the Ease of Access Center

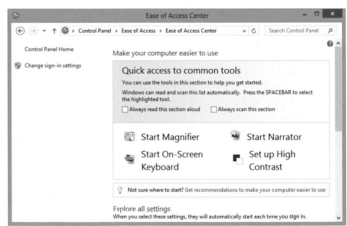

3   Start the main tools – Magnifier, Narrator, On-Screen Keyboard, High Contrast

4   If you are uncertain, ask for recommendations to make your computer easier to use

5   Scroll down to explore all the settings

11 Maintenance

Keep your Tablet PC in its most efficient state by taking advantage of the Mobility and Action Centers, and let Windows Update manage the software. Connect your mobile phone to keep your data in sync. Finally, keep an eye on future developments.

Mobility Center

The Windows Mobility Center provides a single location for settings that are commonly used on Tablet PCs and Laptops, including volume, brightness and battery status.

Hot tip

You can also select Mobility Center from the Quick Link menu (see page 34).

To display the Mobility Center on a Tablet PC or Laptop:

1 Select Search, Settings from the Charms bar and type mobility then tap Windows Mobility Center

2 The Mobility Center opens with tiles for settings appropriate to your system

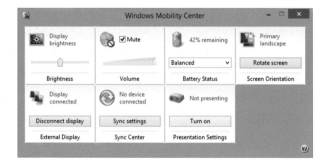

Don't forget

The actual settings covered depend on the configuration of your system. This example is from the Microsoft Surface RT.

3 Drag the slider or tap the button on the tile to apply the setting. For example, Turn on presentation mode

4 For more options for any setting, tap the icon on the tile, and the appropriate options panel is displayed, e.g. tap the Battery icon to display Power Options

The Mobility Center is not normally enabled on Desktop computers, though you can edit the Registry to allow this.

Subject to the specifications of your computer, the settings that you might find in Mobility Center include:

Brightness — Drag the slider to adjust the brightness of your display

Volume — Mute your PC by tapping the check box or drag the slider to increase or decrease the speaker volume

Battery Status — Check your battery power or change your PC's power plan

Screen Orientation — Switch your Tablet PC screen from vertical (portrait) to horizontal (landscape) or vice versa

External Display — Switch to a screen connected to your PC, or change your PC's display settings

Sync Center — View the status of an in-progress file sync or change your settings in Sync Center

Presentation Settings — With this turned on, your PC will stay active and system notifications will be turned off so there are no interruptions

In previous Windows versions the Mobility Center showed the status of the Wireless adapter. This is not the case in Windows 8, even on the Microsoft Surface.

Don't forget

You get easy access to several of these adjustments, when you tap Settings via the Charms bar.

Hot tip

Your computer supplier may provide product specific variations on the contents of the Mobility Center.

173

Action Center

There are various security and maintenance features in Windows 8 and these are monitored in the Action Center. You are alerted by messages on the icon in the notification area.

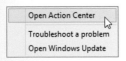

Alternatively, use Search, Settings for action on the Start screen and select Action Center.

1 Tap the icon to see the message summaries, then tap Open Action Center

2 Action Center will warn you when your spyware or virus protection needs installing or updating

3 It may remind you to run a scan using Defender, the antivirus software included in Windows

4 You will be informed if there are problems you have not yet reported to Microsoft

5 Action Center also has links to Troubleshooters and to Recovery tools

Compatibility

Windows 8 helps you deal with older programs.

1 Tap and hold the Alerts icon and select Troubleshoot a problem, then select Run programs made for previous versions of Windows

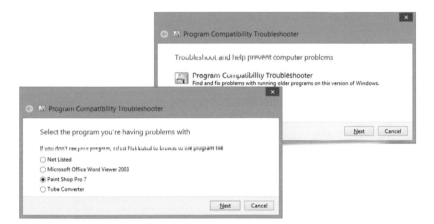

2 Tap Next to find and fix problems with running older programs in Windows 8

3 Select the program and Try recommended settings

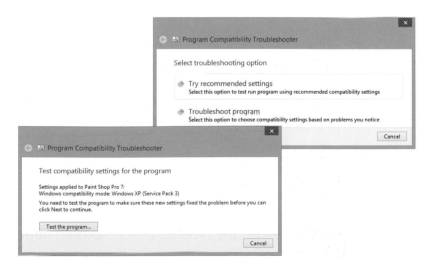

Hot tip

Alternatively, you can Search, Settings for Compatibility, to locate and run the Compatibility troubleshooter.

Don't forget

You must Test the program, to see if the selected settings work, before you can continue and complete the troubleshooter.

Firewall

1 Open Control Panel, select System and Security and tap Windows Firewall

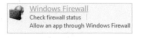

2 Tap Allow a program or feature through Windows Firewall, to view the list of allowed programs

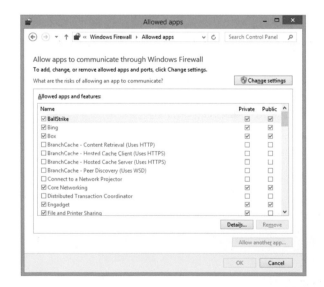

3 Tap Change settings to change or remove allowed features and apps and to enable Allow another app

Defender

1 On the Start screen, search for Defend and select the Windows Defender program

2 Windows Defender opens to display the latest status

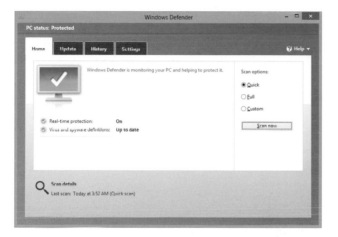

3 Tap Scan now and Windows Defender will carry out a quick scan of your computer and report results

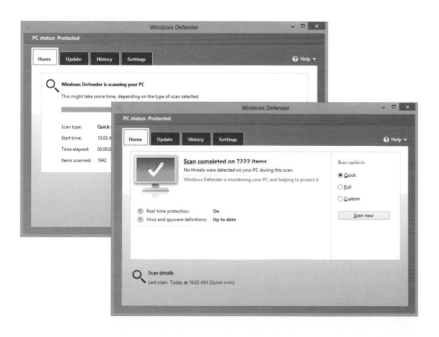

Don't forget

Windows Defender provides protection against malicious software such as viruses and spyware, so you do not have to install separate utilities.

Don't forget

The Action Center may also alert you and offer to run a scan.

Hot tip

Windows Defender also alerts you when spyware attempts to install or run, or when programs try to change important Windows settings.

Windows Update

To review the process by which software
updates are added to Windows 8 computers:

1 Tap and hold the Alerts icon and
select Windows Update, or
open Control Panel, System and
Security, Windows Update

2 Windows displays the status and gives a summary of
the settings that are currently in effect

3 By default you receive updates for Windows only, but
you can Get updates for other Microsoft products

4 Tap Change Settings and you'll see that you get
Recommended as well as Important updates

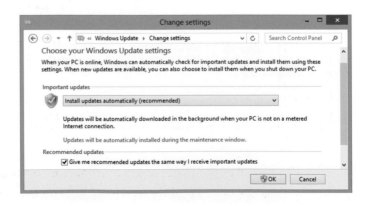

...cont'd

There are some differences for Windows Update as included in Windows RT, in terms of the level of control it offers you.

1 The Control Panel entry does not include the option to Turn automatic updating on or off

2 Windows Update does not offer to Get updates for other Microsoft products or to Change settings

In Windows RT, Windows Update is always turned on, and updates for other Microsoft products are always included. For both versions, updates are installed automatically at 3:00 am by default. To change the update time:

1 Search Settings for maint... and select Change Automatic Maintenance settings

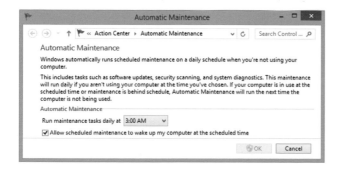

2 Tap the box Allow scheduled maintenance to wake up my computer – the default for Windows RT

Don't forget

Windows Update always installs updates for Windows RT with its pre-installed Microsoft Office, and there's no option to turn this off.

Hot tip

You can check for the latest status by tapping Windows Update in PC Settings.

179

Administrative Tools

You'll find many of the functions that you need to maintain your Tablet PC in the set of Administrative Tools:

1 Open Control Panel, select System and Security and then locate the Administrative Tools entry

2 Note that Windows RT does not offer the option to Free up disk space

3 Tap Administrative Tools to display the Windows 8 tools
or
Windows RT tools

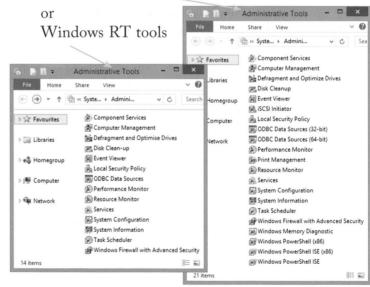

4 There are additional tools available for Windows 8, with some specific to the 64-bit edition

5 Note that the tools Defragment and Optimize Drives, Disk Cleanup and System Information have been moved here from other parts of Windows

Tablet PC Settings

There are some additional functions in the Control Panel for your Tablet PC or Touch monitor.

1 Open Control Panel and select Hardware and Sound

Hardware and Sound
View devices and printers
Add a device
Adjust commonly used mobility settings

2 Tap Tablet PC Settings to calibrate your Touch Display, Touch Keyboard and Handwriting Panel

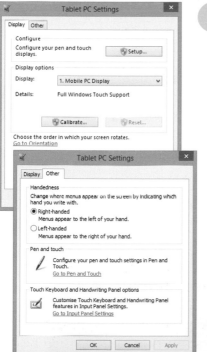

3 Tap Pen and Touch to adjust the durations and the tolerances for touch actions

Don't forget

You'll also find the Windows Mobility Center (see page 172) for all battery-based computers including Tablet PCs.

Don't forget

If there are positioning problems with your screen, you can tap the Calibrate button to recalculate the values.

To provide calibration samples, tap the crosshair each time that it appears on the screen.

181

Hot tip

You can also control the visual feedback that you get when you touch the screen, especially when you use the Tablet PC with a second monitor or projector.

Windows Phone

Even screen capture is similar. On the Surface PC press the Windows key + Volume up. On the Windows Phone press the Windows key + the Power button. In each case the image is added to a Screenshots subfolder in the Pictures folder.

The latest version of the Windows Phone uses the Windows Phone 8 system which is based on the same kernel software as Windows 8 and shares its styling. So when you turn on your phone, you see the Lock screen with live data. Swipe upwards to reveal the tile-based Start screen, and swipe sideways to view and scroll the familiar-looking Apps list.

  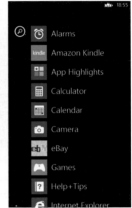

When you attach your phone to your Tablet PC, the ease of connection confirms the family relationship.

1 Plug the USB data sync cable into the phone and then into the Tablet PC, and power up the phone

2 Windows 8 detects the phone and automatically installs the Windows Phone 8 app from Windows Store

3 Start the new app and you'll be prompted to provide a name for your phone and to input your photos

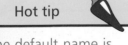

The default name is Windows Phone, but you can change this to something more personal if you wish.

4 The Windows Phone 8 app displays the contents of your phone and transfers all the photos

Hot tip

Tap one of the buttons Add photos, Add video or Add music to transfer files from the Tablet PC to the Phone.

5 The photos copied from the phone to the PC are in From Windows Phone in the Pictures library

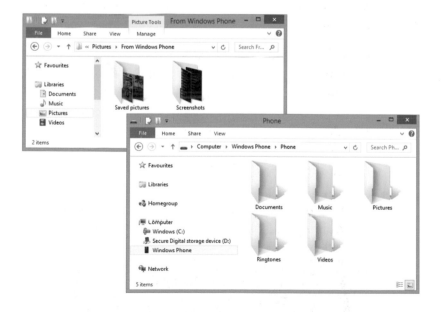

Don't forget

You can copy files directly between the Tablet PC and the attached Windows Phone, from the folders in File Explorer.

6 You can access all the folders on your phone from File Explorer, Computer, Windows Phone, Phone

Desktop App

If your Tablet PC has Windows 8 rather than Windows RT, you have a second option for managing your Windows Phone, using the Desktop app. To download this:

1 Go to **http://www.windowsphone.com/** and search for windows phone app for desktop

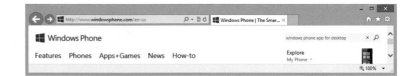

2 Select the web page offering a download for this app

3 Review the requirements and features of this Desktop app, then select the Download now link

4 Run the downloaded file and tap Install then follow the prompts to complete Setup and launch the app

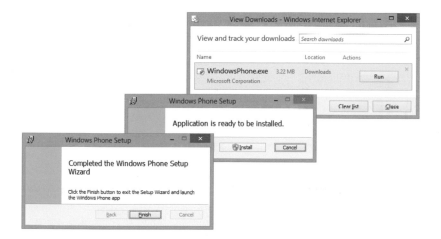

5 The app asks for the phone name and suggests you import photos and videos to the Windows Libraries

6 You can sync all the items for any of the libraries or just specific items, for example an artist in Music

Developments

Don't forget

You can expect Tablet PCs and Windows to undergo major changes, so it is useful to keep in touch with developments. One way to do this is to follow the blogs managed by the teams responsible for making these changes.

Hot tip

Go to the website for your particular Tablet PC and search for any relevant blogs that may be available.

Beware

If you open this web page in the Windows 8 Internet Explorer you are told the site uses add-ons that require Internet Explorer on the desktop.

1 For news and background stories about Microsoft Surface Go to **http://blog.surface.com/**

2 For information about Windows, current and future versions go to **http://blogs.windows.com/**

3 For the latest on Microsoft Office, computer and Cloud versions, go to **http://blogs.office.com/**

Index

J

K

L

M

N

X

Y

Z